GREAT CANADIAN ROMANCES

Love, Scandal, Deceit and Passion

Barbara Smith

First printed in 2005 10 9 8 7 6 5 4 3 2 1

Printed in Canada

The Publisher: Folklore Publishing

Website: www.folklorepublishing.com

Library and Archives Canada Cataloguing in Publication

Smith, Barbara, 1947–
    Great Canadian romances / Barbara Smith.

(Great Canadian stories)
Includes bibliographical references.
ISBN-13: 978-1-894864-52-7
ISBN-10: 1-894864-52-2

    1. Canada—Biography. 2. Couples—Canada. 3. Love—Canada—History.
I. Title. II. Series.

FC25.S638 2005   320.071   C2005-906192-8

Project Director: Faye Boer
Project Editor: Nicholle Carrière
Editorial Intern: Bridget Stirling
Production: Linda Bolger
Cover Image: Courtesy of CP/Abaca Press (Denise Fleming)

We acknowledge the support of the Alberta Foundation for the Arts and the Canada Council for the Arts for our publishing program.

PC:P5

Table of Contents

Dedication

For Bob, of course

Acknowledgements

No one ever writes a book alone, and for this reason I would like to thank a number of people. More than a decade ago, Dennis Mills first suggested that a book of Canadian romance stories would be a fun project. You were absolutely correct, Dennis— thank you. And to Faye Boer of Folklore Publishing, thanks for giving me the opportunity to write this book. Thanks also to Nicholle Carrière for her insightful edits, and to Linda Bolger for laying the book out so beautifully. And, as always the reference librarians at Edmonton Public Library were there with obscure answers when I needed them. Many thanks for your patience and determination in hunting down factoids! And, of course, appreciative thanks to those closest to me, my friends and family who put up with me while I'm distracted by work.

Introduction

NO ONE, NOT EVEN A CANADIAN, CAN COME AWAY FROM a romantic encounter unchanged. Romance transforms us—profoundly. Sadly, all romance ends, at best, with at least one broken heart. Even if the love lasts for a lifetime, the remaining partner is inevitably heartbroken by his or her soulmate's death. Despite those inevitabilities, we still love love.

Georges and Pauline Vanier had such a lifelong romance. Their love was so vast and powerful that it spilled over into every aspect of their lives and left the world a better place. But predictably, Pauline was devastated by Georges' death.

Pierre and Margaret Trudeau's romance began in fairy-tale style. The handsome prince (okay, prime minister) swept the innocent little flower child off her feet, took her home to his palace (well, the official residence in Ottawa, anyway) where they lived happily ever after. Not!

Other relationships might have been romances to the people involved in them, but to outsiders, the situation just looked like a circus. For instance, was there ever a crazier couple than Harold and Yolanda Ballard?

Some affairs of the heart might be improper (Wilfrid Laurier, you strange old duck!), but at least because we're Canadian we do always try to maintain our dignity—well, maybe except when a cabinet minister or two is involved with a German prostitute who might also be a spy!

Did you know that Anna Leonowens, the famous Anna of *The King and I* fame, has a Canadian connection, or that Oscar Wilde's first homosexual lover was not only a Canadian lad but descended from one of our young country's respected leaders?

But, enough hints. Read on and find out for yourself that there is nothing boring about Canadian history—as long as you look in the right places by turning over some hearts and seeing if you can spot the stories of romance underneath. Although Prime Minister Trudeau rightly decreed that the state had no business in the nation's bedrooms, following the romantic paper trails at least to the doors of those bedrooms provides an entertaining slant on Canada's past. Read on and enjoy the history they didn't teach us in school!

CHAPTER ONE

Margaret Sinclair and Pierre Trudeau
Once Upon A Time

She chose her outfit with care. A simple black dress and matching shoes, a double strand of pearls—eminently appropriate for the occasion—her last-ever date with the man she'd loved—and scorned—for most of her life. She looked far older than her years. Had her wardrobe choice aged her? After all, such a stark outfit imposes its own maturity, dignity.

Sadly, no, it wasn't the clothes. On October 3, 2000, Margaret Trudeau was simply and utterly overwhelmed by grief. The man she had adored and distained for decades, the father of three of her sons, was dead. What a long and difficult journey it had been! So many heartbreaks. Staggering to think that 25 years ago on that very date, the couple had proudly welcomed their third son, also now deceased, to the family.

THE LOVE STORY THAT ENDED ON THAT CRISP FALL DAY in a Montréal basilica, began in paradise. It was Canada's centennial year, 1967. The Sinclair family—father, mother and all five daughters—were in Tahiti for their Christmas holidays. Nineteen-year-old Margaret, the second youngest, was sunbathing when a middle-aged man stopped to chat with her. At the time it must have seemed an ordinary, if slightly flirtatious, exchange. But, of course, so many of life's watershed moments seem ordinary at the time.

Joseph Philippe Pierre Yves Elliott Trudeau was 48 years old at the time. He was unquestionably Canada's most eligible bachelor—well educated, well travelled and sophisticated. He dated celebrities, intellectuals—all of them beautiful women. The choices were his. And, he was prime minister of the country.

But the image of that pretty teenage girl at the beach had imprinted itself on Pierre Trudeau's psyche. "I always remembered her eyes," he explained later. And really it's no wonder, because every time the man looked into a mirror he would've seen an almost identical pair of cool, blue eyes staring back at him.

Margaret and Pierre's chance meeting that Christmas also had an effect on Margaret, for she had fallen in love with Pierre. Her parents didn't approve of the man, but then they hadn't approved of very much that the youngster had done, including moving away from home at the age of 16.

Despite her youth, or possibly because of it, it's doubtful that Margaret was ever intimidated by Pierre, although she probably should have been. But she knew very well how to manipulate older men into giving her whatever she wanted—she'd had a lifetime of practice. Her father, politician James Sinclair, had taught her a lot.

Still, in early August 1969, when the phone call came from the prime minister's office asking her out for dinner, Margaret resorted to the stereotypical "What should I wear?" Her standard hippy-dippy garb of sandals with flowing cotton tops and skirts would just not do. By 7:00 PM on the ninth of that month, the 21-year-old was ready for her first date with a man two years older than her own mother. She was dressed modestly in a tasteful gabardine dress. (He wore a yellow ascot! But this was the 1960s.)

The press paid the couple little heed. Reporters were well used to seeing Trudeau dining with beautiful women.

As first dates go, theirs must've gone well because within weeks, Margaret had moved to Ottawa and was working for the government.

The two continued to date, but Pierre saw other women as well. He escorted Barbra Streisand to an official function and was also seen with Liona Boyd, the glamorous classical guitarist. And through it all, his close friend, the intellectual Madeleine Gobeil, was never far off Trudeau's personal radar.

Even though she had already made up her mind that she would marry Pierre, Margaret reacted to all this competition for his time and affections by becoming engaged—to a theology student.

Her tactic was an effective one. Trudeau responded by inviting her to the prime minister's residence at Harrington Lake. It was there that he first mentioned marriage. Margaret pounced on the idea.

And so it was that on the morning of March 5, 1971, Canadians awoke to a surprise. The previous afternoon, the country's oh-so-cool prime minister had married! Daily newspapers carried front-page photographs of the happy couple leaving a church and being showered with confetti. How amazing! Tongues wagged. They fooled us! Of course, the two had been seen together, but no one thought this was a significant relationship. Everyone had assumed they had nothing in common!

How wrong that assumption was.

Although a 30-year age gap separated the two, the newlyweds were actually remarkably similar. Both the bride and groom had been raised in wealthy homes by aloof fathers and dominated mothers. Both were the second-to-last children born to those parents. They had both spent time in far-off cultures (Morocco particularly) "finding themselves." But the most remarkable (and important) coincidence was their physical resemblance to one another. Both had bright blue eyes, prominent high cheekbones and toothy grins. Given the narcissistic nature they both possessed, that mirror-imaging alone could have clinched the deal.

So Canada had its own fairy-tale love story. Surely they had found the way to "happily ever after." But there were huge stumbling stones on their yellow brick road to marital bliss—not surprising really, considering they were also both studies in dichotomy.

By autumn 1975, Margaret had given birth to three sons (Justin in 1971, Sasha in 1973 and Michel in 1975), the first two showing a remarkable sense of timing by being born on Christmas Day. Pierre kept the press pretty much away from his wife for those years.

Each time Margaret emerged from her stone fortress at 24 Sussex Drive, Ottawa, she left puzzlement in her wake. In 1972, she climbed aboard the bus carrying reporters covering Trudeau's election campaign. Margaret informed the journalists that she was an "earth mother" and that she and Pierre were "on different trips."

Less than a year later, the earth mother persona was gone, replaced by a polished-looking political wife. She wanted Canadians to know what a "great guy" her husband was. The strategy worked, or at least helped. Trudeau was re-elected. By then, though, at her own admission, Margaret was no longer in love with her husband.

During the summer of 1974, Trudeau took three-year-old Justin away on a fishing trip, while Margaret headed to Paris in search of a former lover. She couldn't find him. Perhaps to ease her disappointment, Margaret moved on to Crete where she stayed, out of touch with everyone, for two weeks.

Shortly after returning to Canada, she accompanied Pierre to a dinner party in New York. There, over the course of a few hours, she "fell in love" with a man widely rumoured to be Edward Kennedy. It's difficult to know whether any relationship between her and the senator actually existed or was merely a figment of her imagination. Not long after that incident, the Trudeaus were back in Canada, and Margaret became a psychiatric patient. After staying in the hospital just a few days, she checked herself out and returned to 24 Sussex Drive with yet another personality.

Canadian voters watched as a national television broadcaster interviewed a sad, haggard-looking young woman on the grounds of the prime minister's official residence. Margaret spoke in a little-girl voice eerily reminiscent of Jacqueline Kennedy's few televised interviews. Despite the obvious strain that all of these events would've put on her marriage, Margaret was soon pregnant again. Michel was born in October 1975.

Next, Margaret decided to pursue a career as a photographer, declaring that she hoped to become the family breadwinner. After that, the world's children became her focus, followed by ecological concerns. The marriage was nearing its end.

At an official function in Venezuela, she unexpectedly and inappropriately burst into song.

Not long after, Margaret Trudeau uttered her famous declaration: "I'm more than just a rose in my husband's lapel!" She called a press conference during which she rambled nonsensically.

The end had now arrived. Margaret and Pierre separated.

Six years to the day after she'd become Mrs. Trudeau, Margaret was in New York famously partying with the Rolling Stones. When she returned to Canada, partly to be close to her three sons and partly because she really had nowhere else to go, Margaret stayed in a small apartment upstairs at the prime minister's official residence.

From there, in yet another vain attempt to establish a career and hopefully keep herself financially, Margaret took roles in two movies. Both films were so bad that they were never even released. She began to hang out regularly at the discotheque Studio 54 in Manhattan, where an infamous photograph of a panty-less, cross-legged Margaret was taken.

The federal Liberal party reacted with horror. Trudeau, however, ignored the situation entirely. Interestingly, throughout the duration of their marriage, Pierre and Margaret rarely said anything publicly against each other. Trudeau's popularity was waning by that time, but the grace he showed won him some voter sympathy and even grudging respect. Maintaining the (accurate) perception of distance between himself and Margaret couldn't have been easy for Trudeau, but the man not only had his career but also his three sons to think about—and he did.

Margaret's life continued to spiral downwards. She made indiscriminate and unwise "friend-ships." She was also doing cocaine. On May 22, 1979, as Trudeau was conceding election defeat, Margaret was once again on the dance floor of Studio 54. The next morning, she awoke to a dreadful realization—her estranged husband was out of office. This meant that he had to move, and she had no place to live.

Fortunately, her ghost-written book *Beyond Reason* had been released the month before. She bought a small house with the publisher's advance. After kicking her cocaine habit, she created a job for herself as the host of a television talk show.

And finally, in 1984, after a divorce from Trudeau, Margaret remarried.

Although he had an active social life, Pierre remained single for the rest of his controversial and influential years. He raised his sons and most effectively guarded his privacy.

Their youngest son, Michel, brought Pierre and Margaret together again—for Michel's funeral. Pierre was 78 years old at the time and never really recovered from the blow of that tragedy. Margaret's "last date" with the country's former leader was Joseph Philippe Pierre Yves Elliott Trudeau's funeral. He had died at the age of 80.

The romance that had begun on a beach in Tahiti 33 years before had finally ended.

Heartbeats

Canadian author Mazo de la Roche burst onto the world's literary stage with her daringly passionate (for the times!) *Whiteoaks of Jalna* novels. By 1927, her royalties and the money from a prestigious writing award she won that year ensured that she also became independently wealthy. The series of 16 books, written over a period of approximately 30 years, carefully chronicles the details of a fictional Canadian family. This is especially interesting because Mazo was not nearly that careful with the details of her own life.

The woman changed her last name, year of birth and place of birth to suit her needs. But perhaps the most interesting aspect of de la Roche's life was her relationship with Caroline Clement. The two women were cousins, once removed. They were also lifelong companions who loved one another utterly. They remained openly devoted to each other throughout their lives. A daring choice, especially for a public figure such as de la Roche, considering the mores of those years.

CHAPTER TWO

Pauline Archer and Georges Vanier
Nearly Saintly Love

Former Governor General Georges Vanier and his wife Pauline were about as close to being a match made in heaven as you're ever likely to see in the real world. Both were born to affluent, Anglo-French Montréal families at the end of the 19th century. Both felt a deep commitment to serve humanity, and both even considered dedicating their lives to their beloved Catholic Church. As if those similarities weren't remarkable enough, both Pauline and Georges were stately looking people who were exceptionally tall for their generation. (She was six feet tall, he just noticeably taller.)

What a terrible shame it would've been if they had never met!

Fortunately, one day in the summer of 1919, Pauline Archer and Georges Vanier were both having lunch at the Ritz-Carlton Hotel in Montréal. Even more fortunate, a mutual friend was also in the restaurant. He introduced the two, and in doing so, changed the course of history for many needy people.

Just the year before, Georges had returned home from World War I a decorated hero but also an amputee. Despite the loss of his leg, he'd chosen to remain in the military. He was a handsome man and must have cut a dashing figure in his officer's uniform. Pauline, for her part, was a well-educated, striking-looking 21-year-old.

Georges, apparently not one to miss an opportunity, immediately asked Pauline out for lunch the next day. She accepted and, according to her memoirs, the two enjoyed themselves very much. But timing, always so important to a blossoming romance, worked against them. Pauline was scheduled to leave in a few days for an extended vacation in France with her parents.

Georges took the news like the gentleman he was—which somewhat disappointed Pauline. Already sure that this was a man she could fall in love with, she secretly hoped that Vanier was at least a little bit sad that it would be months before they could see each other again. If he was, he didn't let his emotions show, but he did tell her that he would like to give her a small gift before she left. She later told a confidante that the gift was "not quite what she had envisioned." Still, she was deeply touched by the map of France detailing the sites of every battle he'd fought during the war.

As meaningful as that gift might have been, Pauline also hoped that Georges would come to the ship to see her off or, at the very least, send a bouquet and bon voyage wishes. He did neither— or so she thought. As it turned out, he had tried to get away from work to be there at the dock as the ship carrying Pauline and her parents sailed away, but he'd been unsuccessful. And he *had* sent flowers—but to the wrong ship! Sadly, the two potential lovers parted with misunderstandings.

Pauline was hurt, thinking that she didn't mean nearly as much to him as he meant to her. How wrong she was.

Three months later, Pauline's parents hosted a gala reception to celebrate their daughter's engagement to an officer in the French army. Now it was Georges' turn to feel hurt. Even though he'd heard the news shortly after it was announced, he didn't acknowledge it right away, and when he did, his congratulatory message covertly gave away his feelings. He sent a telegram reading: "You will understand some day why I have not congratulated you before now."

Once the initial excitement of her engagement had ebbed, Pauline realized that marrying the man she was engaged to would be a big mistake. After weeks of soul-searching, she broke off the relationship.

The following summer, Pauline was back in Canada and vacationing near the St. Lawrence River. There she happened to meet a man who knew Georges Vanier. She was surprised when he told her that Georges spoke of her often. When the man suggested that they send Georges a postcard together, Pauline agreed.

Georges responded immediately. He had been delighted to hear from her and asked if she could come to Québec City to visit him. Once Pauline's parents had arranged appropriate chaperones for their daughter, they agreed.

From the moment Pauline arrived in Québec, the newly reunited couple were together at every opportunity. They went for lunches, for dinners, for sleigh rides. Everything between them seemed to be going so well—except that Georges had still not proposed, a fact that Pauline noted with lessening good grace. Finally, hoping to force his hand, she told Georges that she'd have to return to Montréal the next day. Perhaps determined not to lose her again, he proposed immediately.

The next day, rather than supposedly travelling home, Pauline took a phone call from Georges asking if, in fact, he really had proposed to her the previous evening. When she assured him that he had, he exclaimed: "Good!"

As a token of their engagement, before giving her the more traditional gift of a ring, Georges Vanier gave his beloved Pauline a small vial of mud! It was a piece of earth that had been stuck to his left boot when he was injured so badly in the war that the leg had to be amputated. Pauline treasured the gift for the rest of her life.

The couple saw each other as often as they could. When they couldn't, he sent flowers—not just to Pauline but to her mother as well. This was clearly a man who wasn't willing to take any more chances with his future!

On September 29, 1921, they were married in Montréal at Notre Dame Basilica (where Céline Dion and René Angelil would also tie the knot 73 years later). The details of the Vaniers' honeymoon would've made a good plot for a romantic comedy. Georges didn't feel confident driving with his artificial leg, so his younger brother, Anthony, acted as their chauffer. Unfortunately for the newlyweds, the young man apparently took his responsibilities much too seriously and rarely left them alone. In order to get any privacy at all, Georges was continually thinking up long, complicated errands for Anthony!

Despite the intrusion, the honeymoon was a success and set the Vaniers' marriage on a long and true course. From 1923 to 1941, they welcomed the births of five children, the oldest a daughter, the rest sons. They also worked tirelessly on humanitarian causes, advocating and acting for children, for the elderly, for the poor, for immigrants, for anyone in need. Their love for one another and their deep religious faith seemed to give them endless energy and drive.

By 1959, the Vaniers had finally begun to slow their pace a bit. Then they received a call from Prime Minister Diefenbaker asking to see Georges. After reminding the former military man that it was the 200th anniversary of that legendary fight between the French and the English, the Battle of the Plains of Abraham, the prime minister asked Vanier if he would be willing to become the country's first-ever francophone Governor General. Vanier accepted the position.

In addition to the couple's other very worthy qualities, Diefenbaker had certainly chosen a stately looking pair to represent Canada in the vice-regal post. Georges was in his early seventies by then. With his neatly tailored white moustache and shock of white hair, he was even more handsome than he had been in his youth. Pauline, too, had a thick mane of white hair, still carried herself erectly and was equally striking looking.

For eight years, the pair carried out their duties with vigour and aplomb. The strenuous life that Georges had led, though, had taken a toll on his health. On the morning of March 5, 1967, Georges Vanier died. He had devoted virtually all of his 79 years to the betterment of humankind.

Pauline Vanier withstood the obligations of religious and bureaucratic services honouring her eminently honourable husband but, as any wife of 46 years would be, the woman was devastated by her husband's death.

She spent her remaining years in France, lovingly working with her son Jean, who had established a unique organization to help mentally challenged adults and children.

Pauline Vanier died there in 1991 at the age of 93.

This exemplary, loving couple is being considered for sainthood.

Heartbeats

Cartographer and explorer David Thompson kept detailed journals during his years of travelling throughout the Canadian wilderness. He would note minute events such as "enjoyed a pipe with the men."

So it was that on June 10, 1799, Thompson recorded: "On this day married Charlotte Small." What an old romantic that man was! Charlotte was 13 years of age. Yet this was a marriage that lasted—and lasted and lasted. David and Charlotte Thompson had 13 children and died within three months of one another in 1857.

CHAPTER THREE

Jamie Sale and David Pelletier
Romance on Ice

Nestled between Edmonton to the north and Calgary to the south lies the pretty little city of Red Deer, Alberta. The more than 50,000 residents have access to virtually every one of the amenities Canadians enjoy—including excellent sports facilities. English is the language most commonly spoken there.

This is where Jamie Sale grew up and began her skating career.

Sayabec is a town of 2000 on the south shore of the St. Lawrence River in Québec's Gaspé Peninsula. It is an area of natural beauty, where camping and fishing opportunities abound. Residents of the town tend to make their own fun. French is the language of choice.

This is where David Pelletier grew up and began his skating career.

SALE AND PELLETIER CLEARLY CAME FROM WORLDS JUST about as different as two Canadian kids can, and yet their career paths not only crossed but merged and ignited.

Jamie Sale was only five years old when her tiny silver skate blade first touched the ice for a skating lesson. Every aspect of the experience captivated her. She loved to perform for an audience, any audience. And she knew how to capture any audience's attention. It was obvious right from the beginning that she had what it took—in spades.

David Pelletier's earliest skating experiences were not as promising. His mother enrolled him in figure skating hoping to make him a better hockey player. There was no artificial ice in Sayabec. Skating classes were held on a patch of ice spread over the rooftop of a building! David hated the lessons so much that he often skipped them to play street hockey with his friends. Not only did he not have any interest in succeeding as a figure skater, but his first coach told his mother point blank that David wasn't a talented skater.

Then Calgary, Alberta, hosted the 1988 Winter Olympics, and the lives of both young skaters changed forever. At nearly opposite ends of the country, Jamie and David each watched in fascination as the greatest Canadian figure skaters performed. Before the skating competitions were over, each of them, probably in common with thousands of young skaters around the world, vowed that they too could make it to the big time.

The utterly amazing aspect to those youthful commitments of Sale and Pelletier was that they actually did make it—together. Better still, they found romance along the way.

Sale and Pelletier began to take notice of one another's careers in 1995. Even though Pelletier had a skating partner at the time and Sale was skating singles, her coach was anxious for the two to meet. They did.

But the meeting didn't work—at all. And so, their lives went on, separately.

By 1998, Pelletier was discouraged enough with his career that he seriously considered quitting. At the same time, two-thirds of the way across the country, Jamie Sale's parents offered her a distressing ultimatum—do something serious about figure skating or quit. Without any knowledge of the other's situation, both David and Jamie decided to take one last stab at making it in the figure skating world.

David found a new coach—who quickly arranged a second meeting with Jamie Sale. This time it worked. It really worked. The chemistry between them electrified everyone, including themselves. With only three months' preparation, the new pair competed at Skate Canada. Remarkably, they won bronze.

Their lives together—on and off the ice—had begun.

For the 1999–2000 season, they chose to skate to the theme song from the movie *Love Story*. There on the ice, in front of the world, they skated a love story. Their performances to that music were so emotionally charged that everyone, including Pelletier himself, appeared to have forgotten that he was already married, that Québec figure skater Marie-Josée Fortin was Mrs. David Pelletier.

Soon the media's comments about David's marital status suddenly became conspicuous by their absence. It was clear that he and Jamie were a pair. The future of Canadian pairs skating seemed to be theirs for the taking. They won competition after competition—and Canadian hearts.

Then came the infamous 2002 Salt Lake City Olympics. Jamie and David were together where they didn't want to be, right in the middle of a judging scandal. After a heart-stopping, and accidental, collision between Jamie and Anton Sikharulidze, the male half of the top-ranked Russian pair, Pelletier and Sale skated their *Love Story* program flawlessly. The 50-year drought for Canadian skaters in gold medals seemed destined to end that evening.

But no one took into account, it seemed, that this was figure skating—where the vagaries of judging were mystifying, at best—and this was clearly not an example of best. As the crowd in the Salt Lake City arena cried out for Sale and Pelletier to be awarded perfect scores, the judges huddled over their desks. Moments later, jeers rang through the building, Jamie Sale began to cry, David Pelletier's jaw tensed and expressions on the faces of experts throughout the rink registered shock.

The Russians had won the gold, the Canadians, silver. A controversy of Olympic proportions erupted. If the name Marie-Reine Le Gougne did not become a household word, the phrase "the French judge" certainly did. Rumours flew. The voting process had been rigged. The French judging federation had accepted an offer from the equivalent body in Russia. If Le Gougne would rate Elena Berezhnaia and Anton Sikharulidze as the winners of the pairs competition, the Russians would vote in favour of Marina Anissina and Gwendal Peizerat, the French ice dancing team.

Olympic officials called a closed-door meeting. Under unprecedented, and almost comical, security measures—the door to the meeting room was sealed shut with duct tape—Le Gougne confessed. The ensuing furor began to overshadow other athletic events. Even Sale and Pelletier, who by this time were suffering from serious sleep deprivation because of the chaos, spoke of the unfairness—not to themselves, but to the other competitors, because the controversy had taken much-deserved attention away from other athletes.

Finally, something approaching justice was done. The International Olympic Committee took Le Gougne's vote out of the mix entirely. This meant that Pelletier and Sale had tied with the Russian pair. A second set of gold medals was struck and awarded—to the Canadian kids who richly deserved them.

And "richly" is somewhat of an operative word in this case, too. Throughout the days following their terribly misjudged skate, the world fell in love with Jamie Sale and David Pelletier. Advertisers all over North America were anxious have the pair represent their products. In the end, the injustice proved extremely lucrative for the young couple.

Eventually, the hubbub died down and Jamie and David's lives began to return to what, for them, passed as normal. All aspects of their relationship, including the romance, had survived a test of utter chaos. Since then, they have retired from the amateur figure skating circuit and turned professional. Although there's been no word publicly about it, presumably David and his first wife have divorced because at Christmastime 2004, he and Jamie became engaged.

The two worlds of Pelletier and Sale—Sayabec, Québec, and Red Deer, Alberta—now seem to have become one.

CHAPTER FOUR

Alma Pakenham and Francis Rattenbury
Architect of Demise

Francis Rattenbury burst upon the city of Victoria, British Columbia, in 1892—a 24-year-old architect with a strong entrepreneurial bent. He possessed considerably more energy than humility, and leaving his homeland, England, meant that he could get away with dramatically embellishing his credentials. And embellish he did. Rattenbury credited himself with designing buildings he hadn't even been connected with—including one that had been built when he was just a child.

All this self-promotion might not have been honest, but it was effective. Rattenbury became the architect of some of Victoria's most prestigious buildings, including the Empress Hotel and the Parliament buildings. He also became a member of the city's social elite. Society matrons adored the handsome, successful young man. Mothers with marriageable daughters were anxious to include Rattenbury in their entertainment plans.

Then, on June 19, 1898, the dashing bachelor shocked everyone who knew him by marrying Florence Eleanor Nunn. Her name was unknown in his social circles. Worse, she was dowdy and decidedly plain.

"WHY EVER WOULD HE MARRY HER?" THE WEALTHY GOSSIPS wondered. Seven months after the wedding that question was answered when Florrie gave birth to a son. But what should have been a joyful occasion was not. Little Frank was born with clubfeet. Doctors predicted he would never walk.

Something of a sick family love triangle developed. The child adored his father, but Rattenbury, perhaps because of the boy's disability, paid little attention to the lad. Florrie, however, lavished every available moment on her son.

Rattenbury threw himself into his career with even greater fervour and determination. His reputation as an architect grew, and he was in great demand. Her husband's success could easily have bought Florrie acceptance into the most prestigious social circles, but she was completely uninterested. She had never been very outgoing, and since Frank's birth had withdrawn even further. By 1900, her whole life consisted of her home and her young, disabled son.

Even Rattenbury was somewhat of an outsider in his own home. The gregarious man conceded this odd set of circumstances and continued to accept many invitations to social functions. Hostesses gave up including Florrie in their plans, because she simply never attended.

Despite the apparent estrangement between Mr. and Mrs. Rattenbury, there must have been something left of the marriage because on May 11, 1904, a second child was born. Rattenbury took one look at his daughter, a tiny pink-and-white bundle and, for the first but not last time in his life, fell head over heels in love. He named the baby girl Mary, after his mother, and proceeded to dote on her as his wife doted on Frank. The combination, of course, was lethal to the already suffering marriage, and soon all pretence of domestic bliss was dropped. Francis and Florrie took separate bedrooms.

For the next 20 years, Rattenbury rode out several career highs and lows, but by then it was clear to all who knew him that he was no longer the fun-loving man who had taken Victoria by storm 30 years before. His miserable home life had taken its toll.

The unhappy situation continued until the last few days of 1923, when the city of Victoria awarded Rattenbury the contract to build a spectacular amusement centre. Shortly after the announcement was made, Francis Rattenbury was sitting in the lounge of the Empress Hotel, which he had designed some 25 years before. A life-changing event was about to take place. No, not the design commission, but an introduction to a beautiful young musician—Alma Victoria Clarke Dolling Pakenham.

Alma was 28 years old. She had been married briefly to a man she adored, but World War I had left her a widow. Shortly after the war, Alma married again. She became a mother and then a divorcee in quick succession.

Francis Rattenbury was twice Alma's age. He was also lonely, successful, married and drank far too much. He was smitten the moment he laid eyes on the sensuous young woman. Their whirlwind courtship began immediately, without regard for Rattenbury's marital status. At first they tried to keep their romance a secret, but soon Victoria's society matrons were once more gossiping about Rattenbury's taste in women.

"Ratz," as Alma dubbed him, didn't care. His unhappiness and celibacy were finally over. Thanks to the sexually aggressive Alma, he was having the time of his life. He was puzzled and offended, though, by his friends' reactions to his new-found happiness. He'd expected that they'd be delighted for him and anxious to include Alma in their numerous social occasions. After all, she was not only gorgeous but had quite a reputation as a musician and composer. But those former friends wanted nothing to do with this new pair. They found Francis Rattenbury a changed man. Some even wondered if Alma and Ratz were dabbling in cocaine or some other kind of drug.

Rattenbury was hurt by their reaction. He was also fearful—fearful that he would lose his beautiful Alma to another, probably younger, man. The thought was more than he could bear. He had to marry her. And he had to do it soon. Besides, he was sure that as soon as he and Alma were married, his friends would include them in the social functions that Rattenbury loved so much.

Of course, first there was that little matter of a divorce from Florrie.

Surely if he begged…And beg he did.

Florrie replied, "No." Ratz begged some more.

Florrie replied some more, "No, no, no, no."

Desperate, Rattenbury set about changing Florrie's mind. He moved out of the house, taking most of the furniture with him. When that didn't have the desired effect, he had the heat and power in the house turned off. Considering that his beloved daughter Mary also lived there, these ploys really showed how determined the man was. Next he began taking Alma to the house, where she would play the piano for hours. That was the last straw for the beleaguered Florrie. She filed for divorce and named Alma as the co-respondent.

Much to Rattenbury's surprise, Florrie also began to play dirty. Part of the divorce agreement stated that he should buy a new house for her. She insisted this house be designed by Rattenbury's former partner, and she chose a piece of land on a hill overlooking her former home—the place where Ratz and Alma would be living.

Rattenbury agreed. He really had no choice. He simply had to marry Alma and resume his lost social life—at any cost.

Only part of the man's dream came true. He did marry his beloved, but even so, no invitations materialized. The couple was devastated. Worse, Rattenbury soon realized that he would likely never work in Victoria again. Fleeing the detritus of his personal life was the man's only hope of salvaging anything of his once-flourishing career. The couple packed up all their belongings and moved to England.

Despite having no income, Ratz clearly didn't expect Alma to run the house by herself. Not long after settling in, they hired 17-year-old George Percy Stoner to help out around the place. The boy had been raised by his grandparents, and when the kids at school made fun of him because he was "slow," the older couple simply kept him at home and sheltered him completely.

The passion that once existed between Rattenbury and Alma had evaporated with the alcohol that Ratz was consuming to excess. A month later, Alma had wangled enough money from Ratz for a trip to London—with George Stoner. During breaks from the hotel, the pair went on shopping sprees. With her unwitting husband's money, Alma bought Stoner a wardrobe of stylish clothes, and Stoner reciprocated—in a way. Using money she gave him, he bought a diamond ring for Alma.

When their stay in the city was over, Alma was happy to get back home. Stoner was not. Back at home, they found Rattenbury in such an alcoholic daze that he barely seemed to remember that his wife had been away. That evening, Alma went up to bed, leaving her husband passed out downstairs.

Not long after, she heard a groan, a horrible sound that sent Alma running to her husband's side. He was slumped at an odd angle and struggling to breathe. There was a large purple mark on the side of his face and a pool of blood beneath him.

Fifteen minutes later, the family doctor stood at Rattenbury's side and Alma was downing whisky. George Stoner was hanging back in the shadows of the room.

"This man's been hit," the doctor surmised and promptly called the police. Before daybreak, Francis Rattenbury, the once great architect, was dead, and his wife was in jail, charged with his murder. Time and time again she changed her story. First she blamed herself for the murder, then Stoner, then impossibly, she blamed Rattenbury's son who was still living back in Canada.

Young Stoner, reflecting his lack of intellectual power, bragged that police would never discover he'd murdered Ratz because he'd been wearing gloves when he'd done the deed.

Word of the sensational case soon reached Rattenbury's old friends in Victoria. Gossipy interest began immediately. British Columbia newspapers covered every gruesome detail of the story and the murder trial that followed.

Stoner, they read, seemed nervous and uncomfortable on the witness stand. Alma, however, was composed, even through allusions to drug and alcohol addiction in the Rattenbury household. In the end, only Stoner was found guilty. Alma was a free woman. Justice had likely been served. Stoner was taken away to jail, while Alma was admitted to a nursing home for care and observation.

A few days later, Alma "borrowed" a small amount of money from an employee at the nursing home and walked out the front gate. That evening, a farmer spotted her sitting and smoking on the bank of the River Avon. As he watched, she calmly put out her cigarette and walked into the river. Then she took a knife and plunged it into her left breast—over and over again. Minutes later, the witness pulled Alma's body to shore.

She had died as dramatically as she had lived. An inquest confirmed that she had stabbed herself a total of six times. Three of those blows had pierced her heart!

After his lover's death, Stoner developed a very different spin on the murder. He claimed that he had taken the murder weapon to the house for innocent reasons. Alma, he said, had found it outside and used it to kill Rattenbury. The young man won a retrial and was sentenced to seven years in jail for his part in the murder.

And so, the romance that began in 1923 in Victoria, British Columbia, ended in Bournemouth, England, as a double tragedy.

Heartbeats

Marguerite Sedilot has held an unusual record for 350 years. And by now, it's doubtful that anyone will ever take the honour away from her—much less want to. You see, on September 19, 1654, Marguerite, of New France, became Mrs. Jean Aubuchon. She was 11 years old at the time!

Did her parents approve of the marriage, you might ask? Not only did they approve, they set the whole thing up in 1643 when Marguerite was just a few weeks old. Fortunately, at the time of the marriage, the groom was an older man—of 20. There's no record of whether or not the union was a successful one.

Compared to Marguerite, Samuel de Champlain's wife was the picture of maturity. Hélène Boulle was 12 years old when she married the great Canadian explorer in 1610. He was 40.

Hélène's parents were pretty forward thinking, though. They insisted the bride could live at home with them until she was 14. As it turned out, Hélène stayed in France with her parents until she was 22. When she finally did join her husband in Canada, she left again after only four years. Despite this, Champlain probably considered his marriage a success because Boulle's parents had provided a dowry of 6000 *livres*, which he used to finance further explorations.

CHAPTER FIVE

Marie-Anne Gaboury and Jean-Baptiste Lagimodière
A Love That Changed Canadian History

In 1792, 12-year-old Marie-Anne Gaboury's life changed forever when her father died. Marie-Anne was in the middle of a cluster of seven children that her widowed mother had no hope of supporting in the French farming village of Maskinonge on the north shore of the St. Lawrence River, just west of Trois-Rivières. The girl was sent to live at the parish priest's home as his housekeeper's helper.

Cloistered away from people her own age, Marie-Anne had no chance to meet eligible young men in her community, so she was still a spinster at the age of 25. She may even have already resigned herself to a lifetime of service when 27-year-old Jean-Baptiste Lagimodière returned to Maskinonge after four years of exploring, fishing and trapping in the wilderness to the northwest. Neighbours in the village threw a homecoming party in Lagimodière's honour and, as luck would have it, that celebration was one of the few social events that Marie-Anne attended.

GOING TO THAT HOMECOMING PARTY NOT ONLY CHANGED Marie-Anne's life but eventually altered the course of Canadian history. Jean-Baptiste began to court the young woman. And she, thinking that he'd returned home to settle down on the fertile land by the river, accepted his proposal when he asked her to marry him. After an engagement of just a few weeks, Marie-Anne and Jean-Baptiste were married on April 21, 1806.

On her wedding day, Marie-Anne presumed that she'd become the wife of a farmer. How wrong she was. Jean-Baptiste had much more exciting plans for himself than years of tilling the soil. He loved the freedom that he'd experienced in the wilds of the West and was anxious to head back out to "the high country" as soon as he possibly could.

Marie-Anne was aghast. She begged her husband to stay at home, but he confessed that he didn't think he had any control over his wanderlust. For a while, she probably considered just staying behind in Maskinonge—at least now she'd have the status of being a married woman—but the idea didn't please her. The parish priest may have been the one who first made the utterly astonishing suggestion that the bride go along with her husband on his travels.

After much thought, the young woman must have decided that her former employer's idea was a good one, and Marie-Anne informed Jean-Baptiste that if he was going travelling, then she'd be going with him. He was horrified. Women didn't go with the men on their trips! Two weeks later, though, they were in a canoe together heading west. They travelled continuously for four months. The Natives they met along the way had never seen a woman of European descent, and they were fascinated by Marie-Anne. As a result, Jean-Baptiste guarded his wife carefully for fear that someone would try to kidnap her.

Even though she was with her husband, Marie-Anne was homesick. By Christmastime, she was also pregnant. On January 6, 1807, the couple's first child, a daughter, was born at a settlement just south of present-day Winnipeg. Marie-Anne was delighted to be a mother and at last began to enjoy her new surroundings—just as Jean-Baptiste announced his plans to pull up stakes and move on.

Once again, he wanted her to stay behind, this time with the baby, but Marie-Anne would have none of it. Despite the fact that she would no doubt have preferred to head east, back home to show off her new daughter, the young woman prepared for the journey farther west to Fort Edmonton.

Over the four winters the Lagimodières spent at Fort Edmonton, they became a cohesive team, even working traplines together. In 1811, when they left that fort to return to the Red River area, they were the parents of three children. But it wasn't until the following year that Marie-Anne finally had what she'd dreamed of from the moment she married

Jean-Baptiste—a home of her own. It had been six years since she'd seen another French woman, and she was delighted to be living among other settlers. Although Jean-Baptiste continued to explore and trap, he always came home to Marie-Anne and their growing family. Neither Jean-Baptiste nor Marie-Anne ever saw their hometown on the banks of the St. Lawrence River again.

In the summer of 1820, their last child, a daughter named Julie, was born. Defying all odds of that era, every one of the Marie-Anne and Jean-Baptiste's eight children—four sons and four daughters—lived to adulthood. The Lagimodières became grandparents to an astounding 64 grand-children, one of whom was Louis Riel, the controversial Métis activist.

And so it was that the relationship between Jean-Baptiste and Marie-Anne that had begun at his homecoming party in Maskinonge so many years before, contributed significantly to Canada's development as a country.

In 1855, Jean-Baptiste left Marie-Anne forever. As a widow, she moved in with one of her sons, where she lived for another 20 years, respected as the great matriarch she had become.

CHAPTER SIX

Johannah and James Donnelly
United They Fell

If the Donnellys—James, Johannah and one-year-old James Junior—were poverty stricken when they left Ireland in 1842, they were poorer still by the time they'd made their way across the Atlantic. They must've been delighted when they found a good-sized piece of prime farmland in what is, today, southwestern Ontario. They must also have been an industrious couple, for James and Johannah Donnelly got right to work erecting buildings, planting crops and having seven more children.

UNFORTUNATELY, THEY'D BEEN TOO BUSY TO ATTEND TO ANY legal details such as buying, or at least renting, the land they had settled on. When the rightful owner sold the property they were living on, the new owner ordered them off his land. They refused to budge, and in the murderous feud that followed, the now-large family became known as the "Black Donnellys."

James Donnelly Senior drew the first blood. During a drunken argument, he murdered a man named Pat Farrell. Now it wasn't just the landowner who was after him, but every one of his neighbours and, of course, the police.

Donnelly ran for cover. For several days, no one saw the man, and so the searchers began to look farther out into the countryside. This meant that James' best hiding place was at home with his faithful Johannah. Besides, he knew his wife would need his help with all the work around the place. Under cover of darkness, James sneaked across his carefully planted fields and back home.

Johannah and the children were relieved to see that James was still alive. They were determined to keep him that way—by any means possible. Together, the couple concocted a plan to keep James hidden—while in plain view. Whenever he stepped outside the house, James was dressed in one of Johannah's dresses!

For the next several weeks, whenever neighbours noticed a woman out working in the fields the Donnellys had been farming, they simply presumed it was Johannah. The ruse worked!

For a while.

The couple's fight to stay together lasted for several weeks before someone began to suspect that the hardworking "woman" tending the crops was not Johannah at all, but her murdering husband. James was arrested, tried, convicted and sent to Kingston Penitentiary for seven years.

Those were tough years for all the Donnellys. Prison in the mid-1800s wasn't a place that would have improved anyone's outlook on life.

And, though Johannah and the rest of the family managed to remain on the farm, by the time James came home again in 1865, the entire clan all had decidedly bad attitudes. It was them against the world—or at least their little corner of the world. Soon, nearby barns were mysteriously burning down. Cattle were found slaughtered, the carcasses left in fields to rot. Wagons were vandalized. Worse, on the nights that these crimes occurred, the Donnellys couldn't account for their whereabouts.

The neighbours decided to retaliate in a very permanent way. On the night of February 4, 1880, a vigilante committee broke into the Donnellys' home. Three members of the family, as well as James and Johannah, died that night. The couple died the way they had lived—together, fighting futilely against overwhelming odds.

James and Johannah Donnelly were undoubtedly a miserable pair, but they were also, in their own misdirected way, unquestionably united and true to one another.

Heartbeats

The devastation of heartbreak can change a person utterly. Sometimes love's loss can even change the course of history.

All of Frederick's hard work was starting to pay off. His medical practice in London, Ontario, was beginning to flourish. Soon, he would be able to marry Edith, the love of his life.

But in 1920, Edith Roach suddenly broke off her engagement to Frederick Banting. The man was crushed. He shut down his doctor's office and accepted a position with an oil exploration company in the Northwest Territories. Then, at the last minute, the company decided that they didn't need an on-site doctor after all. Banting moved to Toronto, where he began working as a medical researcher.

Within two years, Dr. Frederick Banting had discovered that injecting insulin into diabetes patients reversed their symptoms.

In 1923, the man who had intended to practice general medicine in a small southwestern Ontario city with his beloved Edith at his side and then tried to freeze the agony of the heart she broke by moving to the frozen North, instead devoted himself to research and made a discovery that has saved the lives of millions of people all over the world.

CHAPTER SEVEN

Imaginary Romances

At one time or another, it's likely that every person in the world has fantasized about romance. How wonderful it would be to meet and fall in love with an absolutely perfect mate! If such daydreams weren't so common, we wouldn't have nearly the stock of books and movies that we do. These stories, whether we tell them to ourselves, read them or watch them on film, are simply harmless fun—usually. Sometimes, though, fiction and reality become confused, and when they do, the results can be heart-achingly sad.

Castle in the Woods

IN 1903, JIMMY MCOAT BEGAN TO BUILD A HOUSE, BUT NOT just any house—McOat set out to build a castle. It would've been a daunting prospect for anyone, but Jimmy's circumstances made it even more so. He was a small man who lived on a rugged and isolated piece of land at Otter Lake in the equally rugged country of northwestern Ontario.

Despite these conditions, the man toiled at his task nonstop for more than a decade. In the end, he was the proud owner of a log castle. Dennis Smyk, a local resident who is an expert on McOat's castle, explained that the place is "three storeys high, with a four-storey tower and a two-storey kitchen. It was built of red pine logs, some as large as 24 inches [61 centimetres] around. Those logs, when they were green, would've weighed almost a ton."

The castle windows, all 26 of them, were manufactured in the town of Ignace, Ontario. Jimmy picked them up one by one from town and took them home by canoe—a trip of 32 kilometres that included 15 portages! This was a man obsessed with building a dream home—long before such a term even existed.

McOat's neighbours often wondered how he kept going. After all, he was a man in his early 50s when he started this mammoth project! They never wondered, though, why he kept going, for they knew that he was building his castle for the woman who would become his queen. You see, Jimmy was in love, and it was the power of that love that fuelled his extraordinary drive. She, like Jimmy had years before, would soon emigrate from Scotland.

By 1914, the log castle was complete. Jimmy McOat was 63 years of age. Now all he had to do was wait for his beloved to join him in the lovingly constructed home. Jimmy lived in the place by himself for four years, waiting for his love to come to his side. Then, in 1918, Jimmy McOat drowned while he was fishing.

His beloved lass from Scotland never saw the enormous castle that Jimmy had toiled for 11 years to build—probably, sadly, because she had only existed in his imagination.

Cobblestones of Love

When Henry Hoet bought the cottage on the bank of Lee's Creek, in southern Alberta, the previous owners were relieved. They didn't think they'd ever sell the property. After all, the creek had flooded 10 years before, and the land surrounding the little house was still scattered with cobblestone boulders. But to Hoet, those cobblestones were a great advantage. They were an almost endless supply of free building material!

Hoet had come to the Cardston area in 1911. He was an expert craftsman who had worked on both the Mormon Temple in Cardston and the Prince of Wales Hotel in Waterton National Park. All of the man's spare time, however, was devoted to creating a home fine enough for the woman he loved. He would send for her soon.

First though, Hoet had a lot of work to do.

He built the exterior walls from the cobblestones that were so readily available. The materials for the inside arrived a few pieces at a time, from Europe. Only the finest in material and workmanship would do. Hoet carved and installed hundreds of intricate wooden panels for the ceilings and walls. He wired the house for electricity, an unheard-of extravagance in that era, to service the 40 light fixtures he had crafted.

Townsfolk had always considered Hoet to be a bit of an eccentric. He wouldn't tell anyone where he'd come from, though he did mention once that he'd been born and raised in Belgium. As the man toiled away to make his home perfect for his beloved lady, neighbours noticed that he was becoming even stranger. He would work on his house for days on end without stopping to eat or rest. And he began talking to himself constantly as he worked.

Hoet eventually collapsed from exhaustion. He was admitted to a mental hospital, where he lived a long and unhappy life, never recovering from his illness. He died in that hospital on a fine spring day in 1949. No one has ever known whether Henry Hoet was driven mad by the fact that the woman he loved never joined him in the exquisite home he'd toiled to build for her, or whether he'd been unbalanced from the beginning and his beloved had only existed in his own demonized mind.

The fact that Hoet never received even so much as a card or letter the entire time he lived in the house on the bank of Lee's Creek does lead even the most romantic person to conclude that the latter explanation was the case. Whichever, it's heartbreakingly obvious that Henry Hoet was mad for love.

Milli and the King

King Edward VIII's 1936 abdication of the throne to marry Wallis Simpson, the woman he loved, is without a doubt one of the most romantic tales in the world. Perhaps surprisingly, there is a mysterious Canadian love story link to the king.

It all began in 1919. The Great War had just ended, and members of the British royal family were making courtesy visits to the Commonwealth countries that had contributed to the victory. Edward, the 24-year-old Duke of Windsor and Prince of Wales, came to Canada. During his trip, the Prince stopped in the small Ontario town of Galt (now part of the city of Cambridge). Four hours later, after all the formal functions and presentations were over, Edward waved to the crowd and moved on to his next stop. It's likely that Millicent Milroy, a 29-year-old spinster school teacher, was among the well-wishers gathered to bid the prince farewell.

Milli, as she was fondly called, lived her entire life in a simple and quiet way. After she retired, she often ambled about her neighbourhood dressed in shabby clothes. Her small house was never in good repair, and she shared it with a host of cats. Despite her eccentricity, there was an undeniable air of dignity about the woman, and to listen to her stories, it's no wonder. Millicent Milroy firmly maintained that she and the Duke of Windsor had not only met during his brief visit to Galt, but that they had fallen in love and later married!

While there is absolutely no proof that the two did meet, much less marry, there were those who knew Milli and thought she was telling the truth. Their belief was supported by fact that over the years, Milli regularly received envelopes in the mail from England. Some folks even went so far as to speculate that there were cheques in those envelopes—perhaps hush money of a sort.

Funny how no one ever guessed that the envelopes simply contained letters from relatives or a pen pal! That would not have been nearly as exciting.

Be that as it may, by the time Milli died in 1985 at the age of 90, she had made all the necessary arrangements for her own funeral—including the tombstone she wanted placed on her grave. That marker is still standing today. The epitaph reads in part: "Millicent Mary Maureen Marguerite, wife of Edward VIII, Duke of Windsor."

Was she or wasn't she? We'll never know, but the tale is a delightful addition to Canada's cache of romantic stories.

The Lady with the Lamp

In the mid-1800s, Reverend John Smithurst faithfully served a parish in Elora, a pretty little town in southwestern Ontario. Smithurst lived alone and had apparently never been married. That wasn't to say, though, that he'd never been in love—he certainly had.

Many years before, when he was a young man in England, Smithurst had fallen hopelessly in love with a woman whose name would soon become known all around the world. The object of John's affections was none other than the famous nurse, Florence Nightingale. But sadly, the two knew they could never marry because they were first cousins. They decided on the next most romantic option—they would each devote themselves to the service of humankind.

And so they did.

Florence Nightingale, of course, became the woman behind the nursing profession as we know it today. She served selflessly during the Crimean War (1853–56) and is credited with having eased the suffering of thousands of injured soldiers, saving the lives of hundreds more and revolutionizing the field of nursing. She never married.

John Smithurst's life of service was not quite so remarkable, but he too remained single for the rest of his days. He and Florence apparently realized that they had found their soulmates in one another, but fate, in the form of a too-close family connection, would not let their romance flourish.

Today, the only object that remains of this bittersweet tale of romance from Canadian history is a silver communion service—two chalices and a serving dish—owned by Smithurst's former church. The plate is engraved: "To Reverend John Smithurst, a very dear friend, in grateful recognition of his many kindnesses."

Smithurst acknowledged to those closest to him that the silver service had been a gift from his much-loved cousin, Florence Nightingale. It was, he explained, a token of her affection for him and a celebration of the love they had known.

That story certainly is a romantic tale and has become a legendary part of Canadian history, but it's doubtful that it's true. Nightingale scholars have never found any trace of a man named Smithurst anywhere in her family tree.

After the Crimean War, Florence Nightingale became revered by people around the world. It's likely that Reverend John Smithurst was simply a lonely bachelor who took that reverence very personally and on into the realm of a romantic fantasy.

Heartbeats

Valentine's Day cards can be many things. They can be sweet, they can be funny, they can be inappropriate or they can be welcome. Rarely, however, is such a card mysterious. But for Meryl Dunsmore, every February 14 brought a mystery.

The first card arrived in 1928, when Meryl was just a teenager. It was signed from "Your secret admirer." The young woman was surprised but simply presumed that the card was from some boy she'd gone to high school with, one who was too shy to identify himself.

If she was correct, then the boy may have been shy, but he was also very persistent. For the next four decades, Meryl continued to receive anonymous Valentine cards. The greetings arrived despite two marriages and subsequent name changes as well as six moves. Through it all, she had never had any idea who her secret admirer was. Judging from all the different postmarks, though, it was a fair bet the man was a traveller. The cards were mailed from different countries all over the world.

Then, in 1968, the expected card didn't arrive. Meryl was puzzled. There really was nothing she could do, though, as she had no idea who her secret admirer was, let alone how to contact him. That summer, she received a note from Paris. Her secret admirer explained that he had been sick on Valentine's Day and so hadn't been able to send a card.

Another 20 years passed. Each February, greetings arrived regularly. In 1988, the card was postmarked from Sweden. The verse read: "An old-fashioned wish is always in style, when it comes from the heart and is sent with a smile." It was the last Valentine's Day card Meryl Dunsmore ever received. She died that summer.

On the morning of her funeral, a beautiful array of yellow mums and white lilies lay by the front door of the funeral home. The following words were written on a card tucked into the bouquet: "Rest in peace, my Valentine." One of Canada's great, and mysterious, romantic stories had ended.

CHAPTER EIGHT

Yolanda MacMillan and Harold Ballard
Sticks and Stones

Pet names have long been the hallmark of couples in love.

In 1924, long before his involvement with the Toronto Maple Leafs hockey team, 21-year-old Harold Ballard met 17-year-old nursing student Dorothy Higgs. As a play on her surname, Ballard immediately dubbed her "Jiggs Higgs." The spur of the moment nickname stuck for life. In turn, he informed Dorothy that he was often called "Old Smiley."

Jiggs Higgs and Old Smiley began to date. They must've loved dating one another, because they did so for a very long time—17 years to be exact. Much to her minister father's chagrin, Dorothy was 34 years old by the time Ballard proposed to her. They were married a few months later. By this time, Harold was well entwined with Maple Leaf Gardens and the Toronto Maple Leafs. And now, in addition to the moniker Old Smiley, some of his friends called him "Pal Hal."

THE NEWLYWEDS SETTLED INTO A NICE HOME IN AN UPSCALE west-end Toronto neighbourhood. Three children, a daughter and two sons, were born in quick succession from 1945 to 1947. In keeping with the times, Mr. and Mrs. Ballard formed the "perfect" little household. Harold earned the money to support the children financially, while Dorothy supplied the love and understanding to support them in every other way.

Harold maintained his womanizing. Dorothy maintained her dignity.

Then, in 1965, the unthinkable happened. Jiggs Higgs, the Ballard-family pivot, was diagnosed with breast cancer. Harold suddenly realized that his days of neglecting the only person he'd ever truly loved might soon be over. He was devastated. Together they fought the illness as long and as hard as they could.

But they lost.

On December 2, 1969, Harold Ballard buried his "best friend," the beloved Jiggs Higgs. To his credit, he had devoted himself to Dorothy for the last four years of her life. Some might say it was too little too late for the mother of his children, the woman who had stood by him from adolescence onwards, but that was simply how it was.

On July 30, 1983, Harold Ballard turned 80 years old. By that time, he had become many things that he hadn't been while his beloved Jiggs was alive. He was old. He was lonely. And he was an ex-con, having served time for fraudulent use of Maple Leaf Gardens funds.

This was the Harold Ballard that Yolanda Babik MacMillan arrived at Maple Leaf Gardens to see. Ballard invited her into his quarters. Had she not thought to bring him a birthday cake, the course of their futures might have run very differently, but Yolanda had no doubt done her homework. She knew very well that Pal Hal had an incredibly difficult time turning down either sexy women or sweet food. By the time she left his office that summer's day, the relationship that would last the rest of his life was underway.

Yolanda's exact age was a bit of a mystery, but it's certain that she was at least 50 years old at the time. Sportswriter Dick Beddoes commented that at that point in her life, she was "as demure as an iron foundry." Like Ballard, she had also served jail time for white-collar crime.

As Harold's physical health began to decline, so did his mental health. Those who had once called him Pal Hal now referred to the elderly man as "Weird Harold", and Ballard, in turn, called Yolanda "Yo-yo," probably with more derision than affection given that he also called her a "lunatic."

Yolanda was also playing a name game. She had legally changed her surname to Ballard. When she talked to reporters, she frequently referred to "my Harold."

When Harold had a heart attack while the couple was vacationing in Florida, the problems between Ballard's adult children and Yolanda began in earnest. The press dubbed them the "Battling Ballards." Bill Ballard, Harold's older son, was especially vocal in expressing his dislike for, and distrust of, his father's companion.

The old man's health continued to worsen, and on July 22, 1988, Ballard underwent heart surgery. When the operation took longer than expected, rumours began circulating that Weird Harold had died on the operating table. The rumour wasn't true, but the price of stocks in Maple Leaf Gardens went up. As he recovered in the hospital's intensive care unit, the shares dropped again.

In the meantime, Yolanda, using the name Mrs. Ballard, had taken a room in the same hospital. Bill Ballard was furious. On one occasion in the hospital, the bickering between the Ballard factions elevated to the point that the nurses called the police. Peace was restored for the sake of the other post-surgery patients on the floor.

Back at Maple Leaf Gardens, locks were changed so that Yolanda couldn't get into Ballard's suite. Then notices ran in Toronto newspapers advising merchants that neither Harold Ballard nor Maple Leaf Gardens would be responsible for debts incurred by Yolanda. Despite the implications of those actions, the lovebirds (or odd ducks) remained together until Harold's death on April 11, 1990, at the age of 87.

Like an elder statesman or a religious leader, Ballard's body lay in state at Maple Leaf Gardens.

Weird Harold had become so unpopular that his death had caused the price of Gardens shares to shoot up again. Afterwards, he was once again remembered as Pal Hal.

Ballard's three adult children succeeded in curtailing Yolanda's involvement with their father's funeral. She was allowed an hour with his body before being asked to leave the building. Yolanda and the press were banned from the funeral.

In his will, in addition to his good wishes, Ballard specified that the woman he'd called a lunatic would receive an annuity of $50,000 a year until such time as she married. Yolanda was mortified at the paltry sum. She fought, successfully, to have the sum increased.

In 2005, Yo-yo was approximately 75 years of age. She has not remarried and still uses the name Ballard.

CHAPTER NINE

Amanda Reid and Rick Hansen
No Average Canadian

On June 27, 1973, until eight o'clock in the evening, Rick Hansen was about as average a 16-year-old Canadian kid as you could ever want to meet. He and a friend were hitchhiking home from an extended fishing trip. At a curve in the road, the man driving the truck they were riding in lost control of his vehicle.

The next words Hansen spoke were: "I can't move my legs." Those few words would shape the rest of his life.

Rick Hansen would never again be an average Canadian.

It was fully seven months before he made it home from that trip. And when he did, the teenager had a lot of difficult adjustments to make.

DESPITE THOSE DIFFICULTIES, OR BECAUSE OF THEM, IN 1975, Hansen entered his first sports competition as a "disabled" athlete. In 1979, he began competing in wheelchair marathons. A marathon, by anyone's definition, is an endurance test. But for an athlete whose body is already challenged, the long distance is even more gruelling. Hansen was completing a last-minute training run before heading to Boston for the prestigious Boston Marathon when, as he put it, he "hit some turbulence." Going downhill at 50 kilometres per hour, he was thrown from his chair.

He was lucky—in a way—all he needed to recover from the horrible accident was another extended stay in the hospital and a highly skilled and devoted physiotherapist—Amanda Reid, by name. She began to work with Rick, and soon they began to see improvements—in Rick's injured wrist and in his outlook on life. Then Amanda began coming to see him in the hospital for extra treatments—on her days off. It was in that hospital, after one of those extra treatments, that the two shared their first kiss. Maybe not the most romantic setting in the world, but it was the only one available to them.

Once Rick's injury healed, he returned to his sports career, and Amanda continued hers as a physiotherapist. The two kept in touch and even went out on dates together every now and again.

By this time, Rick had an idea bouncing around in the back of his mind. He knew it was a bit crazy. Even so, he couldn't seem to shake it. He and Terry Fox had been friends. He had greatly admired Terry's courage and determination in running the Marathon of Hope. Perhaps, Rick thought, he could do something similar. What if he tried to go around the world in his wheelchair? Surely if he did, the journey would draw attention to spinal cord injuries and raise money for research.

But what about his life? Rick knew he'd be gone from home for more than a year, maybe even two years. That might have a very bad effect on one particular part of his life—his love life. By then, Rick Hansen knew that he loved Amanda Reid. What he didn't know was whether or not he could he bring himself to be away from her for that long. It could be risky. After all, she was an attractive young woman. Who was to say that she'd be willing to wait for him? As frightening a thought as that was, it was a chance he was going to have to take because Hansen knew that he had to at least try to complete this crazy goal he'd dreamed up for himself.

As good and powerful ideas often do, Rick's dream almost immediately began to take on a life of its own. Before he knew it, the supports required for making such a mammoth and complex journey had come together. On March 21, 1985, the young man and his entourage rolled away from the Oakridge shopping mall in Vancouver. The "Man in Motion" tour had begun.

The plan was that Amanda would accompany Rick to the U.S.-Canada border. Then she'd return to her job and her life, while the man she loved wheeled himself around the world.

That was the plan, anyway.

The tour hadn't even left Washington State before Rick's wrist started to give him serious trouble—almost as much trouble as his emotions were giving him. He missed Amanda terribly. It was possible that she could fix both problems. Rick phoned her, and after the two had talked for a while she, perhaps naïvely, asked a life-altering question: "Do you want me to come down?"

Three days later, Amanda Reid was in Portland, Oregon, ready to go the distance with Rick.

Romantic relationships meet stresses. It's a fact of life. Some relationships survive, some don't. But the stresses Rick and Amanda would put theirs through were horrendous. They were going be together 24/7 for months and months and months. Worse, they'd be cooped up in a motor home with a minimum of six other people, while Rick attempted an unimaginably demanding feat. Tough circumstances for a romance to blossom under!

By Christmas, they were in New Zealand. It was their first Christmas together, and they were a long way from home. It was summer, which, for a pair of Canadians, was just plain wrong. And they were physically and mentally exhausted. Amanda bought a plant and declared that it would serve as their Christmas tree. How festive.

Over the next nine months, the couple endured everything that the journey threw at them. At various times, and sometimes at the same time, they became extremely ill. They were robbed. They were angry, cranky, tired and fed-up. But by September 30, 1986, they had made it back to

Canada. They were in New Brunswick. They were also secretly engaged.

At least they thought their engagement was a secret! Both Rick and Amanda had naïvely presumed that with all the strains the team surrounding them had to cope with, no one would notice anything so small as a ring on the fourth finger of Amanda's left hand. How wrong they were. By the time they each phoned home to tell their parents the happy news, almost everyone in Canada had already heard it on the radio!

At their next stop, journalists peppered the pair with questions. It seemed that people were at least as intrigued by this marvellous love story as they were by the story of the Man in Motion tour itself. One of the most frequent questions the young couple had to field was a thinly veiled inquiry about Rick's ability to father children. They answered patiently that, yes, they did want a family, and no, there was no reason why they shouldn't expect to have one. In his memoir, Rick pointed out that no one would have thought of asking able-bodied people such a question. Touché, Mr. Hansen.

As happy as the romantic news was, the two still had, literally, many miles to go.

The couple spent their second Christmas in Wa Wa, Ontario—a much more romantic setting than their first Christmas. Their temporary home was a log cabin with a fireplace, an unbeatable view of Canadian wilderness in the winter and a real

Christmas tree. Unfortunately, Rick was battling a bladder infection. A smart-aleck friend back in Vancouver at least injected some humour into the situation by predicting a newspaper headline: "Rick Can't Go Wee-wee in Wa Wa."

The humour was needed because the location in northern Ontario was roughly where Terry Fox had been forced to abandon his Marathon of Hope. The coincidence was at the back of everyone's minds. Besides, though they were well into Canada, it's an awfully big country. They still had more than 3000 kilometres to go, and it was winter. In order to complete the journey, Rick would have to wheel across the rugged terrain of the Canadian Shield in –20°C temperatures.

Fortunately, the Man in Motion team was beginning to actually see the results of their efforts. The fund they'd been collecting for had reached an incredible $5 million. Cities were planning alterations to sidewalks, public buildings, schools and sports facilities to make them more accessible to people using wheelchairs. Rick Hansen had succeeded in bringing much-needed attention to the obstacles that people in wheelchairs face every day.

In Alberta, as they wheeled north from Calgary to the province's capital city, Edmonton, they stopped at a jail, where Rick spoke with a disabled inmate about the fact that the correctional centre had just been renovated to be wheelchair accessible.

Rick and Amanda were presented with a ball and chain, a gift that was symbolic on two levels—the difficulties disabled people face and the fact that Rick's bachelor freedom would soon be hobbled.

On May 22, 1987, Rick, Amanda and the rest of the team reached the Oakridge shopping centre in Vancouver. They had done it. And they had done it together. Over a period of two years, two months and one day, Rick and Amanda had travelled over 40,000 kilometres (nearly 25,000 miles) and had raised more than $25 million for spinal cord research. Perhaps, though, the fact that their love for one another not only survived but strengthened on the journey is even more amazing than any number of kilometres or dollars could ever be.

On October 10, 1987, at Vancouver's British Columbia Club, Amanda Reid and Rick Hansen were married. The bride looked gorgeous in her ankle-length white dress adorned by a single strand of pearls. The dashingly handsome groom wore a tuxedo and used crutches rather than a wheelchair. They stopped briefly after the service to chat with the fans and reporters who had gathered to catch a glimpse of the newlyweds.

"I'm very lucky," Rick told the crowd. He kissed his wife and then added: "This is forever."

After the reception festivities, which included a five-tier wedding cake, the couple left for another trip, this one strictly for pleasure—a month-long honeymoon in the South Pacific.

Today the Hansens are the parents of three daughters. They live in Richmond, BC, and continue to run the Rick Hansen Man in Motion Institute and Foundation.

And, according to all accounts, they continue to enjoy their great Canadian romance.

Heartbeats

Passionate kisses have long been a staple of Hollywood movies, and the first-ever onscreen kiss was actually half Canadian. In 1896, May Irwin of Whitby, Ontario, locked lips with an American actor whose name has long since been forgotten. Whoever he was, hopefully he and May were fond of one another, because the filming process for that one little token of romance took five full days! Presumably they took breaks to brush their teeth!

The movie's title certainly wouldn't win any awards for subtlety. It was called *The Kiss*. No word on whether or not the film was a box office hit, but it certainly earned a place in cinematic history. That half-Canadian buss really started something!

CHAPTER TEN

Royally Romantic

An Enduring Illicit Relationship

How perfect! A heart-shaped pond in memory of an illicit but deeply enduring romance.

This would be a remarkable story no matter who the lovers were. But the fact that she was a French aristocrat and he was destined to become the father of England's longest-reigning monarch makes the tale even more intriguing.

ENGLAND'S PRINCE EDWARD, THE DUKE OF KENT, WAS BORN in 1767. While he was still hardly more than just a boy, it became obvious that Edward loved the ladies. By 1790, his passion for romance had caused Edward's father, King George III, to banish the over-eager young man from England. The king no doubt thought that Gibraltar would be a safe place for his randy son to wait for the ugly gossip about his French girlfriend's ill-thought-out pregnancy to fade away. Of course, King George couldn't have known that he was only succeeding in sending his son to fall in love again—this time forever.

Edward's new love, Alphonsine Julie Theresa Bernardine de St. Laurent de Montgenet, the

Baronne de Fortisson, was seven years older than the prince, and she was rumoured to be experienced in the ways of love. She was also clever and pretty. Better still, Cupid had apparently arranged for her to be in Gibraltar at the same time as Edward!

Now, all this might sound like a recipe for a happy relationship, except for one small but significant matter. Julie, as she was known, may have been a member of the French aristocracy, but Edward would never be free to marry her—she was a commoner. Despite that insurmountable problem, the two were rarely apart. Then in 1791, when King George ordered the young prince to Acadia and Lower Canada, Julie went with him.

The lovers lived together happily and openly. There were a few members of that pioneer society who refused to accept Edward's consort, but for the most part the couple functioned as though they were married. No one who knew them ever, for a moment, doubted their love or devotion for one another. Even the governor of Nova Scotia, John Wentworth, admired Julie, and he and his wife Frances frequently invited the couple to dinner parties.

As the years went by, many aspects of life changed. Edward and Julie's relationship, however, remained rock solid. In 1794, they moved to Halifax near where Governor Wentworth had built a small home. The Prince took such a liking to the house that the Wentworths named it "Prince's Lodge" and were honoured to have the couple live in it together.

This union might have happily gone on forever except that Edward was suddenly needed back in England—to produce an heir to the throne. In 1818, after Edward had lived with Julie for half his life, the broken-hearted man answered his royal family's call. After setting up a trust fund for Julie, he left her to do his royal duty. He married Her Serene Highness Mary Louisa Victoria, the widow of a German prince. One year later, the future Queen Victoria was born. The year after that, Edward died, never having seen his beloved Julie again. When Julie heard of Edward's death, she wrote a letter of condolence to his widow, who was said to have been deeply touched by the woman's thoughtful gesture.

What became of Julie herself is largely a matter of speculation. Some say she stayed in Canada, where she died at the amazing age of 106. Others believe that she returned to France—either to join a religious order or to live quietly near family. Despite the clandestine nature of her relationship with the Duke of Kent, Julie has not been forgotten. There is a street in Halifax named after her, and on the grounds of Prince's Lodge, where she had lived happily for so many years, is the small, heart-shaped lake known as "Julie's Pond."

A Royal Romp

Edward's brother William also enjoyed the Wentworths' hospitality while he was in Halifax—especially that of the Governor's wife! Not long after 41-year-old Frances Wentworth was introduced to Prince William, who was then in his early 20s, the two began an affair. The couple didn't do too much to hide their activities, but most of the people in Nova Scotia, including Frances' husband, Governor Wentworth, simply turned a blind eye to the carry-on until the relationship had run its course.

Princess Louise and Reverend Robin
A Canadian Body of Evidence?

Every family has at least one family legend. For the most part, they're harmless stories that have been handed down through the years—possibly as inconsequential as just exactly how big the trout was that Grandpa took out of the lake when he was a young man. One family, the Lococks, have lived for nearly a century with a very much more dramatic tale about one of their grandfathers.

The Locock legend includes illegitimacy, a suspicious death and the possibility that they are descended from royalty! We shall begin this strange tale in a strange place—the middle.

On December 13, 1907, a Montréal railway worker made a grisly discovery. There, lying beside a section of train track, was a corpse. Identification on the body indicated that the remains were those of one Captain Henry Locock. Police determined that Locock had no relatives in Canada. They were no doubt relieved to be able to ship the grisly find to his next of kin in England. The family buried their loved one at a cemetery near their home.

They may not have known the reason for Henry's death, but they did know why he had been in Montréal. Henry Locock had long suspected that he was a royal love child. He had gone to Canada hoping to find the man he thought was his father—the Reverend Robin Duckworth. You see, Locock was convinced that his mother was Princess Louise, Queen Victoria's fourth, and some say favourite, daughter.

Henry was born in December 1867, delivered by Sir Charles Locock, Queen Victoria's personal gynecologist. Immediately after his birth, the infant was adopted by the doctor's family and raised as a Locock. As a child, little Henry played with Queen Victoria's grandchildren—and might well have been one of those grandchildren himself.

Princess Louise was 19 years old when Henry was born. She'd been madly in love with Reverend Duckworth, a man described as her "spiritual adviser"! Earlier in 1867, Queen Victoria had sent Duckworth off to a posting in Canada while the Princess went into seclusion. A few months later, the Locock family welcomed their new addition.

A suspicious series of events? Henry Locock apparently always thought so. He frequently shared those suspicions with his own six children who, if he was correct, would then also be directly descended from royalty.

In the early 1900s, Locock decided to set sail for Canada to see if he could find Robin Duckworth. Presumably, that quest was less daunting to the man than simply staying in England and approaching Princess Louise! No one knows for certain if Henry's mysterious death in Canada had anything to do with his equally mysterious birth, but the saga continues to plague the Locock family.

In March 2004, Nicholas Locock, Henry's grandson, tried to lay the old rumours to rest once and for all. He applied to have his grandfather's body exhumed and tested to see if the DNA matched another descendant of Queen Victoria's. His request was denied—twice. It seemed as though Princess Louise, Reverend Duckworth and possibly Henry Locock had taken the truth with them to their graves.

As fate would have it, Princess Louise also spent a few years in Canada, though certainly not with her former lover. In 1871, the Princess was married off to John Douglas Sutherland Campbell, the Marquis of Lorne. Seven years later, John A. Macdonald selected the marquis as Canada's fourth Governor General.

The appointment was seen as a brilliant move both politically and personally, because it reinforced the tie between Canada and the British monarchy while also serving to remove the marquis from London, where he was prone to having embarrassing affairs with British soldiers. Not surprisingly, he and Princess Louise did not have any children.

Poor Princess Louise Caroline Alberta. If her love child, her only child, had been killed in Canada, then hopefully the fact that Canadians named a province, a lake, a town and a mountain after her helped ease the sense of association at least somewhat.

A Mysterious Relationship

Romance is an intense and wonderful state to be in and to behold. Romantic tension can be equally marvellous, and sometimes the slightly elusive aspect of that tension can make the power even stronger. When a pair of actors have that tension between the two of them, it always makes their love scenes so much more believable. Richard Burton and Elizabeth Taylor had it in *Cleopatra*. Barbra Streisand and Kris Kristofferson had it in *A Star is Born*, Michael Douglas and Sharon Stone had it in *Basic Instinct*. And way back in the 1950s, Yul Brynner and Deborah Kerr definitely had it in that fabulous old musical *The King and I*.

The Rodgers and Hammerstein production *The King and I* was based on the true story of Anna

Leonowens, a British divorcee who took a job as governess to the King of Siam's 60-some children. No one knows for certain if she and the monarch were ever romantically involved even though Anna wrote extensively about her years in the exotic land. It's generally accepted by people who have studied her writing and know the texture of those times that Mrs. Leonowens was never one to let the truth get in the way of a good story.

Two years after she retired from the king's court in 1868, Anna moved to Canada to live with her daughter. She lived the rest of her life in Canada and died in 1915. Anna Leonowens' body is buried in Montréal's Mount Royal Cemetery.

Heartbeats

Oh, how we love love!! We even love to read about love, and no one knows that better than those romantic folks at Harlequin Enterprises. Since 1949, this giant Canadian company has published 117,200 different books, all of them revolving around the theme of love. When they add up all the copies of each one of those titles (and they do add them up!) Harlequin finds that they've printed and shipped more than 5 billion books. And their love line just continues to grow. As of the year 2005, the company produces more than 100 new titles each month!

CHAPTER ELEVEN

Émilie Lavergne and Wilfrid Laurier
Love So Strange

Ah, Wilfrid Laurier—an enigma to be sure. We know he was Canada's prime minister from 1896 to 1911, and that even though he was often controversial, his term in office is held in high esteem to this day. What we don't know, though, is what on earth his relationship with his partner's wife was all about.

EVEN AS A YOUNG MAN, LAURIER WAS TALL AND DISTIN-guished looking. He dressed with great care and wore his curly dark hair in a long, flowing style. He had a powerful speaking voice and a charismatic manner. Like his father before him, Wilfrid Laurier was irresistible to women. And he knew it!

As a student at McGill's law school, Laurier boarded with a wealthy Montréal family named Gauthier. As luck, or Cupid, would have it, a young woman named Zoé Lafontaine also lived there. The two liked to sit together at the piano for hours on end. Laurier would sing, and Zoé would accompany him. She was smitten. She was also patient! For seven long years, Zoé waited for the handsome young man to ask for her hand in marriage.

But he didn't, even though by that time he was well established in a rural law practice and had begun to dabble in politics.

Then, in May 1868, a telegram arrived at Laurier's office. The family he had lived with in Montréal, and where Zoé Lafontaine was still living, was ordering him to "come at once." Laurier boarded the next train bound for the city. He had no sooner set foot inside the Gauthiers' home than he realized what the problem was. Zoé had accepted another man's proposal—and had been sobbing ever since. The Gauthiers knew that Laurier was the only one who could solve the problem. And he did. Less than two weeks later, Laurier and Zoé were married in Montréal. Oddly, he returned to his adopted hometown that evening—alone. It seems he had an important court case early the next morning.

A few days later, Zoé, along with her piano and a few belongings, arrived to begin her new life as a married woman. A few years later, when Laurier won a local election, Zoé added politician's wife to her set of roles. Life was good—almost perfect.

If only there wasn't such gossip about the fact that they were still childless! People said it was Laurier's earthly punishment for his stance against the Church's involvement in politics. Others whispered that Laurier was impotent—or even gay! Although in that era, the word applied was more frequently "pervert." In odd opposition to this murmur campaign, Laurier was mobbed by women whenever he gave speeches.

Through it all and as he progressed from local to federal politics, Laurier maintained his law office in partnership with his good friend Joseph Lavergne. The arrangement was a convenient one because not only were the two men close, but Zoé Laurier had become friends with Émilie Lavergne. This friendship was no doubt all well and good, except that there was one more relationship in the mix.

Every morning at 11:00 AM, as regular as clockwork, Wilfrid Laurier would rise from his desk and say to his partner: "Joseph, if you will permit, I will go talk with your wife." Odd as it may seem, Joseph apparently always did "permit." The routine, and therefore the relationship between Laurier and Émilie, his partner's wife, went on for years.

Laurier supporters maintained that the two were friends only. His detractors professed otherwise. Then, in 1880, Émilie gave birth to a son. She named the boy Armand. Young Armand looked very much like his mother. He also, though, bore a striking resemblance to Wilfrid Laurier's distinctive appearance. Tongues wagged. A local gossip columnist at the time had a field day with innuendos, constantly referring to Laurier's "friend." The journalist also called Émilie "Canada's Lady Chesterfield"—a reference to the woman who was supposed to have been British Prime Minister Benjamin Disraeli's lover.

None of the people intimately involved in the complicated set of friendships between the Lauriers and the Lavergnes ever commented publicly. Some have wondered if Laurier might even have been secretly pleased to have people talking about his possible infidelity instead of his possible impotence or homosexuality. Certainly, if there were secrets to be kept, the four people involved kept those secrets well.

Laurier only ever uttered a single regret about his life and that was that he "did not leave a son." Does that statement counter the evidence of Armand Lavergne and his physical similarity to the former prime minister, or did he mean that he didn't leave a son with the Laurier name? As for Armand, the question of who his father actually was followed him throughout his life. Once, presumably after being told again how much he looked like Laurier, the young man lashed out, saying that regardless whether his father was Joseph Lavergne or Wilfrid Laurier, he had a heritage to be proud of.

In 1963, 64 years after Laurier's death, the Lavergnes' nephew, Renaud Lavergne, produced a stash of 41 letters written by the prime minister to Émilie Lavergne. These letters spanned the years from 1891 to 1893. Renaud explained that his aunt, Émilie Lavergne, had given them to him just before her death in 1930 at the age of 82.

In 1989, historian Charles Fisher published the letters in a book entitled *Dearest Emilie: The Love-Letters of Sir Wilfrid Laurier to Madame Emilie Lavergne*. The letters are fascinating. They all appear to be written in code. The word "friend" is used over and over again. No one's full names are mentioned—initials are used instead—and each note is "signed" only with the initials "W.L." Émilie's name is notably absent.

Not one letter opens with anything like a greeting to her. As a matter of fact, in a letter written on May 21, 1891, Laurier immediately begins to complain that he hasn't had a letter from her recently. He writes: "to an anxious heart…this is most distressing and there will be no rest for mind and heart until I have heard from you." The man was clearly suffering from the predictable heartache a lover suffers when he or she is worried that there might be trouble in paradise.

Laurier's wording in his letters is undeniably intimate—"dear, ever dearer friend," "my heart clings to this paper," "I am proud of your affections," "with a full heart," "eternal affection."

The warmth of his words and the frequency of the letters between Émilie and Laurier are strong evidence that even if there wasn't a physical association between the two, their relationship was unquestionably intimate. To this day, historians and biographers continue to disagree on just exactly how intimate the relationship between Sir Wilfrid Laurier and his partner's wife actually was.

The details of the Laurier love mystery will probably never be known and maybe that's as it should be. As part of his legacy, this great Canadian leader left behind a mysterious love story.

Heartbeats

Looking for love? You'll find it northeast of Saskatoon, near Tobin Lake. Yes, that's where the tiny village of Love, Saskatchewan, is located.

For most of the year, Love is just a sleepy little hamlet. Come the first two weeks of February, though, the pace picks up. Canadians with love in their hearts and romance on their minds send envelopes containing Valentine's Day cards to the post office there. The cards are then re-routed so that the lucky (and loved!) recipients receive words of love postmarked "Love."

CHAPTER TWELVE

Gerda Munsinger and Pierre Sevigny
Our Very Own Scandal

How very un-Canadian! A sex scandal on Parliament Hill? It happened! And news of the intrigue-laden affair rocked the nation while making headlines around the world.

March 4, 1966—Justice Minister Lucien Cardin had taken as much abuse about a particular issue as he could. Opposition Leader John Diefenbaker's attacks had gone on long enough. Cardin popped two tranquilizers, rose to his feet in the House of Commons and shouted that Diefenbaker had no right to criticize considering "Dief the Chief's" handling of the "Monseignor" case.

Silence fell in the House—for a moment. Then pandemonium rose. What was Cardin talking about? "Monseignor"? Had something happened involving the Catholic Church?

Who knew?

At least one member of Parliament probably suspected he knew exactly what Cardin was referring to, and he wasn't happy with the realization.

LATE IN THE SUMMER OF 1958, ASSOCIATE MINISTER OF
National Defence, 41-year-old Pierre Sevigny, was
introduced to an attractive young woman. Despite
the 12-year age gap between the two, she and
Pierre were immediately drawn to one another—for
very different reasons.

The woman was attractive—a former beauty
queen who spoke with a slight German accent.
Best of all, she acted as though she'd never met
a man quite as attractive and exciting as Pierre,
probably because Sevigny had what Gerda Munsinger found excitingly attractive in a man—
wealth and power.

For the next three years, Gerda and Pierre were
an item.

Now, this might have been fine except for a few
pesky realities, the first one being that Pierre was
a married man and a father to boot. Secondly, he
was an elected official and privy to confidential
government matters.

And it gets worse. Gerda Munsinger was a
potential security risk. When she'd applied to enter
the United States, they'd turned her down cold—
something about her once having been arrested in
Germany, possibly for spying.

Despite her history, in 1955, Gerda Munsinger
arrived in Canada to live. Her first job here was
waiting tables. But she was an ambitious sort and
within months was working as a secretary. By
1956, the woman, then in her late 20s, must have

fully utilized all her saleable proficiencies, for she had successfully steered herself into Montréal's fast lane. Her means of support at that time was described as "mysterious" but was sufficient for her to enjoy vacations in Florida and ski trips to Europe. Once she was seen at a nightclub with former heavyweight boxing champion Rocky Marciano.

Soon Gerda began telling people that she was friends with influential government representatives. One name that she often included in her list of friends was then Associate Minister of National Defence, Pierre Sevigny.

Sevigny came from a prominent Québec family. He had served with valour during World War II and had been so seriously wounded that medics had been forced to amputate one of his legs.

After the war, Sevigny continued to serve his country, but in federal politics as a Conservative. On the day he first met Gerda Munsinger, Pierre Sevigny was a cabinet minister. Soon he was able to add "adulterer" to his list of identifiers.

Of the two people involved in the Sevigny-Munsinger affair, Gerda might have had fewer concerns. Pierre had to maintain a carefully constructed image of respectability. In addition to being inordinately proud of his family name and history, the man had his standing in the community as an elected federal official to consider. Any hint of immoral behaviour would have meant trading all of that for abject disgrace. Sevigny apparently decided that such high stakes gambling was worth the risk.

Gerda may also have been shuffling an assortment of roles. She had a history of possible involvement with the Russians, and her Montréal apartment, which Sevigny paid for, was in the same building as a "trading company" known to be a front for Soviet spies. Nothing was ever proven, but that "coincidence" eventually came to support the belief that all the while Gerda was in Canada, she was working for the enemy.

The couple seemed to be able to put aside all their stresses, though, and enjoyed three good, solid years of illicit love. Gerda often showed off a ring that she said Sevigny had bought for her in Mexico. She also acknowledged visiting his apartment in Ottawa and returning the hospitality in her paid-for Montréal apartment. And, if you'd been a Canadian taxpayer during the time of their tryst, you too would've helped fund the couple's jaunt to Boston aboard a government-owned aircraft.

But the occasion Gerda enjoyed the most was a banquet and dance she attended in the late 1950s. Sevigny was not able to escort her to the gala event at the Windsor Arms Hotel in Montréal. Pierre's wife of 20 years always accompanied him to official functions. Gerda's escort for the evening was a nameless "businessman." Despite that slightly less-than-romantic arrangement, Gerda delighted in attending a party with Prime Minister

Diefenbaker and most of his cabinet. She even told a reporter that there might be photos of her and Sevigny enjoying a spin around the dance floor that evening.

The lovers succeeded in keeping their affair pretty much a secret—while it was going on. After a presumably satisfying, three-year-long, part-time union, and on the advice of his boss, Prime Minister Diefenbaker, who had by then learned of the affair, the minister and his mistress went their separate ways. When the Conservatives lost the next federal election, Pierre Sevigny left politics and returned, literally and figuratively, to home and hearth.

Gerda, pleading homesickness for Germany, left Canada.

It wasn't until March 1966, when that Liberal cabinet minister bellowed his slightly mispronounced version of Gerda's last name in the House of Commons, that the affair suddenly became public knowledge—and a potential national security crisis.

A representative from Prime Minister Pearson's office was sent to the Parliamentary Press Gallery to brief anxious reporters. He incorrectly corrected Cardin's pronunciation to from "Monseignor" to the misspelled "Munzinger" and also gave the incorrect first name as "Olga." He then explained that the accusations hurled in Parliament that afternoon were based on charges of illicit sexual relations and implications of espionage. The reporters were told that the man in question had been a member of Diefenbaker's Cabinet and that the woman involved had since died.

Parliament Hill reporters sharpened their pencils, eagerly anticipating a titillating change of pace. The fact that it was then 1966 and the love affair had taken place from 1958 to 1961 would do nothing, they were sure, to dampen the public's fascination.

Each of the former members of the Diefenbaker Cabinet denied being the minister implicated. Those who had been involved perhaps clung to the delusion that the name "Olga Munzinger" would never be corrected to read Gerda Munsinger, so they could go on maintaining their innocence.

Pierre Sevigny, who demonstrated a most convenient dedication to speaking only the absolute literal truth, declared he had "never heard of Olga Munzinger."

While the woman in question was still thought to have died, and even before "Olga Munzinger" had been properly identified as Gerda Munsinger, the name "Olga" was routinely prefaced in the newspapers with the word "buxom." It remains unclear how the reporters had determined the woman's chest size.

Ralph Allen, managing editor of the *Toronto Star*, along with reporters Robert Reguly and Robert McKenzie, were suspicious that "buxom Olga's" demise was far too convenient. Let others determine who the cabinet minister involved in the love affair might be—they set about finding the alleged spying mistress herself. Alive.

And they did.

Gerda's first words to Robert Reguly pretty much gave away the farm. "Perhaps this is about Sevigny?" she asked as she ushered the reporter into her apartment. Munsinger showed amazing composure and restraint under the circumstances. She allowed a 15-minute chat with her unantici-pated visitor before declaring that she was expecting other company and couldn't spare Reguly any more time that evening.

The next day, the *Star*'s bold headlines boasted: "STAR MAN FINDS GERDA MUNSINGER." Below was a sub-headline that read more like a tabloid than a respectable Canadian daily. "In a chintzy apartment in Munich, the girl at the centre of Ottawa's sex-spy scandal talks of life in Canada…" Reguly's story continued: "I was at the door of her apartment within three hours of my landing at Munich Airport. She answered the questions she wanted to answer and left me to guess the rest. And the rest was plenty."

Poor Gerda—the games of love were over. Now the word games, largely at her expense, were beginning. Her hair colour was described as "a dye job" that had "not the greatest effect." Her figure was initially "shapely" but later "she has no bust to speak of at all and skinny legs." So much for buxom. Despite the fact that Gerda was consistently referred to in the press as a "girl," the March 14, 1966, issue of the *Toronto Star* states that

"Gerda has seen better days. She's 37 now and a lot thinner than she was." (Which begs the question of how the reporter could know this.)

Gerda's memory soon became as foggy as Sevigny's. She refused to discuss the private moments of her long-ago relationship. She would only admit to having known Sevigny socially, adding that they were often together. Canadians were aghast at the revelations.

After the *Star* ran its interview with Gerda, Sevigny (with his wife and family at his side) admitted to a scrum of reporters that he knew her but echoed Gerda's disclaimer about their relationship being "purely social." He went on to say that he found her a pleasant individual and that he had enjoyed her company "a few times."

He couldn't, however, remember giving Munsinger the ring that she displayed as a gift from "my Pierre." When questioned about flying to Boston with Gerda, Sevigny was unable to recall ever having travelled with her. The man could not even remember being inside her apartment, though he did distinctly recollect having "bumped into her" at a bar in Ottawa. Given all of his protestations, it's hardly surprising that, when accused, Pierre Sevigny immediately denied being the member of Parliament alleged to have been secretly and incriminatingly photographed on Gerda Munsinger's bed.

The nastiness between the Liberals and the Conservatives, Canada's two main political parties, meant that Gerda and Pierre's secret was destined from its start to eventually hit the fan. A common tryst had exploded into international news, even though it might more accurately be classified as international gossip.

The possibility that national security had been endangered justified the intense and widespread interest, especially for those who normally credited themselves with being above discussing cheap hearsay. In truth, the public was as fascinated then by a scandal as it is today. The media knew this and made the most of it. The affair that had kept Pierre and Gerda amused for something less than three years kept the public amused for something less than three months.

The day after *Star* reporter Robert Reguly discovered Gerda, she disconnected her doorbell and telephone in order to accommodate her promise to grant the *Star*'s request for an exclusive interview. Those precautions were necessary considering that nearly 200 journalists were soon milling about Gerda's door, and others were telephoning for interviews.

You have to wonder just how cooperative the woman would have been if she'd known some of the comments that were going to be reported in the *Star* under the guise of news. While one of the newspaper's reporters helped Gerda with chores by drying dishes while she washed, another observed that a painting in Munsinger's apartment was not very good quality.

A caption under a head-to-toe, front-page photograph of Gerda pointed out that "some of her glamour has vanished," while the accompanying article reported that during the interview she was "chewing tranquilizers" and "sipping Löwenbrau." Slightly stoned or not, Gerda consistently and hotly denied that her love affair with Pierre Sevigny had caused any threat to national security.

Despite this denial that anything newsworthy had occurred, an international media circus had begun. A German tabloid magazine reportedly paid her nearly $50,000 for the exclusive rights to her life story. Even the staid Canadian Broadcasting Corporation jumped into the fray. Producer Don Cameron proclaimed that by the time they'd tied the terms of the television interview down he "...wasn't sure whether we'd sold the CBC to Germany or arranged for [interviewer Norman] DePoe to marry Gerda." Be that as it may, on Tuesday, March 15 (coincidentally the Ides of March), 1966, Canadians finally had their first animated glimpse of the woman whose love affair five years earlier was responsible for the current upheaval in their government.

Despite the controversy swirling around him, former cabinet minister Sevigny kept a long-standing obligation to speak at a Knights of Columbus meeting. There, perhaps buoyed by the standing ovation he received upon entering the meeting hall, he implored this gathering of fellow white, middle-aged, middle-class males to see his side of the situation.

"How on earth do you expect any man to go into public life when he can be smeared until the cows come home?" Sevigny begged, in a hopefully rhetorical question. "What is happening to me is terrible. This whole affair is an inadmissible intrusion into my private life," he continued with self-righteous bluster.

Mrs. Sevigny and her private life also became the object of unwanted attention. Through it all, publicly at least, she remained the picture of dignity, even retaining her sense of propriety when uninvited television crews arrived late one night. She told them that she could not possibly think of going on television as she wasn't properly dressed and her "hair wasn't done."

Canada's publicly funded television and radio broadcaster may have been drawn into the chaos, and respectable daily newspapers may have stooped to tabloid reporting, but our political leaders never lost sight of the fact that beneath all the gossip there remained a serious governmental concern.

After a few months, however, Canadians were more than ready to leave the grisly details of the "love story" between Pierre Sevigny and Gerda Munsinger well behind them in order to prepare for 1967, Canada's 100th birthday.

But Canada would never be the same again. As political humorist Art Buchwald commented: "Canada can now be considered a major power. She rates because she has had a major sex scandal."

Heartbeats

Georges-Étienne Cartier (1814–73) was one of our Fathers of Confederation. He was also quite an unconventional character! He once challenged an opponent to a duel. The dispute ended when Cartier shot a bullet through the other man's hat!

Cartier was a brilliant parliamentarian who argued passionately against Canada becoming part of the United States. He also loved to party.

No wonder the woman Cartier loved was also extraordinary.

Luce Cuvillier was 11 years older than Cartier. Like him, she loved the complex games of politics and cared little for propriety. She shocked members of society by smoking cigarettes and wearing pants. Most of all, though, she shocked people simply by loving Cartier because Luce Cuvillier was not Georges-Étienne Cartier's wife. Dour, strait-laced Hortense Fabre was Cartier's wife. Luce Cuvillier was wife Hortense's first cousin.

And Luce Cuvillier was also Georges-Étienne Cartier's lifelong lover.

CHAPTER THIRTEEN

Mildred Lewis and John Ware
Romance on the Range

"John Ware, the Negro cowboy." That's how Canadian history has recorded one of its most vibrant characters. Of course, the term must be viewed in context, and in the early 1900s, nothing derogatory was intended because John Ware, a giant of a man, was greatly admired by all who spoke of him.

THE FACTS OF WARE'S EARLY LIFE ARE A MYSTERY. IT'S LIKELY that he was born into slavery in the United States, and even more likely that he spent a lot of time around horses. We do know that Ware first saw the Canadian Rockies while he was on a cattle drive. Once he saw the ruggedly beautiful countryside, he knew that this was where he wanted to spend the rest of his life. He immediately set about making himself part of the community around High River, Alberta, about 60 kilometres southwest of Calgary.

One day, when John was in Calgary shopping for supplies, he happened to meet the Lewis family. Daniel and Charlotte Lewis had recently arrived from a predominantly black settlement in southern Ontario. They had a number of children, the eldest of whom was 19-year-old Mildred.

Not long after John and Mildred first laid eyes on one another, it became apparent that they would like to meet. The locals wasted no time in becoming cowboy-cupids, and before long, John Ware had accepted an invitation to the Lewis' home for dinner. Not to be too obvious in their matchmaking, the hosts also invited other friends, the Hansons.

After a delicious meal, Dan Lewis suggested that his guests might enjoy a bit of fresh air in his horse-drawn wagon. With warnings not to stay out too long, that the sky looked like rain might be coming, the Hansons, John Ware and Mildred Lewis headed out for a ride. The four were enjoying themselves so much that the time and the miles passed quickly. Before they realized it, they were a long way from the Lewis' home, and the sky had darkened ominously. John turned the wagon around and warned the other three that he'd be driving the horses hard in order to get back to the house before the storm hit.

Seconds later, a sword of lightning lit up the sky, and a clap of thunder shook the wagon. There was little in life that frightened John Ware, but electrical storms certainly did. They terrified him. Now, though, he couldn't let his fear get the best of him. He had to get everyone to safety. Standing and driving the horses as hard as he could, John focussed everything he had on getting back to the Lewis home. He was making good progress when a second crack of thunder sounded from the heavens, and lightning eerily lit the sky for measurable seconds. The wagon shook and then stopped with a tremendous jolt. Badly frightened, shaken and bruised, the four people stared in disbelief at the ground in front of them. The lightning bolt had hit and killed the horses.

John jumped down from the wagon, and using every bit of strength he could summon, he un-hitched the carcasses from their harnesses. Then, at a trot, Ware began to pull the cart and its three riders back to the Lewis' property, where Mildred's mother waited anxiously.

When they finally came into sight, Charlotte Lewis could hardly believe her eyes. The horses were gone. Only John Ware's enormous strength had powered the wagon, with the three people still in it, through the electrical storm, across the deepening mud and back to safety.

By the time everyone had calmed and warmed themselves by the fire, Charlotte Lewis realized that she had lost a part of her daughter during that storm. John Ware had clearly won Mildred's heart.

The two were wed on February 29, 1892.

In the early spring of 1903, Mildred Ware wasn't well. She hadn't been well since the birth of her last baby the year before. To make matters worse, the child himself was sickly. It seemed that baby Daniel was never long without some sort of a sickness or another. John hated to leave Mildred and the children alone when she was doing so poorly, but he had to get to Calgary and buy the medicine that the doctor said she needed.

John rode through a pelting rainstorm as fast as he dared. When he reached the town of Brooks, John left his horse and boarded a train for the city. By the time he got to Calgary, the rain had changed to snow, and the winds had increased. John made his way on foot to the drugstore. Then, with the brown bottle of vile-smelling liquid safely in an inside pocket, the man began his long trek home.

When he got off the train in Brooks, tiny white granules of blowing snow blinded John. He made his way by memory to the livery stable where his horse was tied. He threw the saddle on his horse's back and led the animal from the warmth of the barn. But for the first time in John Ware's life, he was not able to get a horse to do what he wanted it to. Try as he might, Ware could not get that horse to walk out into that storm. He soon realized that it was hopeless to keep trying. He turned back, handed the frightened animal's reins over to the stable hand and set out on foot. He would walk the 20 kilometres through the blizzard, back to his homestead where Mildred and the children were waiting for him.

John trudged, one heavy footstep after another, his face and hands thankfully numb, well beyond hurting. For miles and hours he pushed on blindly. Nothing existed for the man except the cruelly stinging, icy snow and his determination to get home. His mind was blissfully blank. If he'd understood the situation he was in, even John Ware might have panicked. One moment's hesitation out there in the middle of a prairie blizzard would have brought sure death. It seemed as if he would walk forever through the endless snow.

Then, without warning, his foot hit something solid. The jolt threw him off balance and he fell forward. Thrusting out one frozen hand to cushion his fall, John didn't feel the wire fence rip into his flesh. He only knew that his heavy woollen mitt was torn and that he had fallen, but not to the ground.

Groping under the snow to help himself up, John discovered what it was he had fallen against. It was a cow. Dead, poor thing, blinded by the snow, driven into the fence by the wind and now frozen solid. The discovery jarred John terribly. By now he had few defences that the cattle did not, but thankfully, one of those was the ability to reason. He wiped the snow from the cow's body until he found the brand, and as he did, John uttered thanks to the heavens. The dead animal had belonged to his neighbour. This meant he wasn't far from home. If he just followed the fence line, he should be able to see his own place in no time.

Checking to see that no harm had come to Mildred's medicine when he'd fallen, John set out again. Not many minutes later, he saw a light in the distance. On he trudged, by now so exhausted that he stumbled and fell with almost every step.

In his badly stressed mind, he could already feel the warmth of his cabin and Mildred's arms around him. Moments later, John Ware laid his eyes on the loveliest sight he had ever seen—his Mildred and their children. The family was reunited. John had walked through a blizzard for seven hours to ensure that fact.

If this story of love was a work of fiction, it would end here, with everyone's future happiness assured. Sadly though, real life rarely works out that well. Little Daniel died before his third birthday, and Mildred, who had never fully recovered from the child's birth, let alone his death, died not long after. John was devastated.

He took the other children to live with Mildred's mother, but then found the loneliness completely unbearable. He brought one son back home to live with him. And it was that boy who watched in horror as his father, that giant of a man who was known for his ability as a rider, was thrown from the gentlest steed the Wares owned when the animal tripped in a badger hole and fell forward. John struck his head on the horse's saddle and died instantly. A truly remarkable Canadian love story had ended.

Today there are no descendants of John and Mildred Ware. Only one son ever married, but he and his wife had no children. Janet, the Ware's firstborn, lived well into her 90s, but she remained single. When asked why she hadn't married,

Janet explained that she'd never met a man she could respect the way she respected her father, the legendary John Ware.

Heartbeats

Sometimes, some of us can control our romantic inclinations. World-renowned Canadian painter Emily Carr (1871–1945) acknowledged in her memoirs that as a young woman she had fallen in love with a man from her hometown of Victoria, BC. When the opportunity came for Emily to move to London, England, and attend art school, she forced herself to fall back out of love with that same man.

One day, Emily was in a London park and saw a peacock with his full plumage extended. Watching the bird strut about, she apparently decided there and then that all men were conceited and that she would simply never fall in love again.

As far as anyone knows, the artist kept the vow she had made to herself. There is no indication that she ever had another romance and she certainly never married.

CHAPTER FOURTEEN

Céline Dion and René Angelil
Romantic Music

The large and boisterous Dion family lived in a small Québec town. All 13 children were talented musicians—which really wasn't too surprising. They had inherited their abilities from their parents. The family thoroughly enjoyed entertaining themselves (and probably every neighbour within earshot!) by making music together.

On March 30, 1968, the couple's 14th and last child was born. Her voice and musical talent suddenly made the gifts of all the others seem ordinary. Everyone in the Dion household recognized that little Céline possessed something very, very special. Her voice was as clear as a mountain spring, and even as a child, she could scale an astounding five octaves.

One day, before this little songstress had celebrated her 13th birthday, a family member recorded her singing a song that their mother had composed. Not having any knowledge of the professional music business or how to approach it, they simply sent the demo tape to an address they found on the back of a record cover.

THE SONG REACHED RECORD PRODUCER RENÉ ANGELIL—IN more than one way. Legend has it he wept as he listened to Céline Dion's beautiful voice for the first time. Even though she was just 12 years old and didn't speak a word of English, he immediately signed her to a contract.

Despite her undeniable talent, Angelil's new client was not, at first, an easy sell. No one except René was willing to take a chance on a child, especially one who spoke only French. Undaunted, the man worked to promote his protégée's career within the province of Québec. Céline's mother travelled along as a chaperone wherever the gigs happened to be. René mortgaged his house to get the cash necessary to make the trips. Céline dropped out of school. They were all determined that nothing would come between Céline and her music.

And this is how the aspiring star's teenage years went. But soon it seemed as though everyone's efforts and sacrifices were going to pay off.

By 1988, when she was 20 years old, Céline Dion and René Angelil finally admitted to one another that, despite the 27-year age gap (and his two previous marriages), the two were in love with each other. It was another very productive, profitable and loving six years, however, before they married. By that time their joint efforts and talents had made Céline Dion an international singing star.

On December 17, 1994, in Montréal's beautiful old Notre Dame Basilica, 500 guests witnessed a truly Canadian couple exchanged vows. Those present had been instructed on even the smallest details of their attendance at the ceremony. Dress was strictly "black tie" for the men and "long gowns" for the women. There were to be no gifts, thank you. In lieu of wedding presents, guests were asked to make a donation to the Québec Cystic Fibrosis Association. That request was in memory of Céline's niece Karine.

The dressmaker put the finishing touches on Céline's $25,000 wedding dress just hours before the bride walked down the aisle. Opinion is divided on whether the ceremony was tastefully extravagant or over-the-top tacky. Whichever, it was definitely a production. The bride arrived at the church with her father in a Rolls Royce accompanied by a police escort. Her eight sisters carried her train. René was already there. As planned, his arrival had been heralded by trumpets. Céline's brothers were his groomsmen. An hour later, the once-little girl with the angelic voice and the man whose belief in her never faltered had become husband and wife.

This fairy-tale love story that began, as fairy tales often do, so humbly, continues. The couple invited 235 of their closest friends to attend an elaborate vow renewal ceremony on January 5, 2000. The ceremony was held at Caesars Palace in Las Vegas—the home of Celine's extravagant (even by Las Vegas standards) nightly show.

The singer's only deviation from her professional commitment to that show was to appear in an ad for Air Canada, in which she proved that anyone, even someone as beautiful as Céline Dion, looks bad wearing clothing made of polyester.

René Angelil and Céline Dion's marriage has proven to be an enduring love story. Their union has seemingly been solid, despite the normal trials that life can throw at any of us, including child-birth (their son René-Charles was born on January 25, 2001) and René's life-threatening illness, as well as a few stumbling blocks that only those in the limelight seem to attract.

Heartbeats

Lucy Maud Montgomery (1874–1942) was raised by her stern, humourless grandparents. But that upbringing didn't dampen Maud's romantic inclinations. She was constantly cre-ating stories in her imagination and assigning whimsical names to places around her beloved Cavendish, Prince Edward Island.

When Maud was 16, she left her grandpar-ents' home and went to live with her father in Prince Albert, Saskatchewan. Once she was there, it didn't take long for one of her school-teachers to fall in love with her. Maud would have none of it, though. She promptly and firmly told the man "no" when he proposed marriage to her.

Shortly after that, the young woman returned to the Maritimes and started her career as a teacher. She also fell in love for the first and only time in her life. The man was a farmer who lived near Cavendish. Sadly, Maud's grandmother was a widow by then and in poor health. Maud felt she couldn't leave the elderly woman who had raised her. Less than a year later, the only man L.M. Montgomery ever loved died from the flu.

When Maud was in her early 30s, she became engaged to a minister—Reverend Ewan Macdonald. He had agreed to keep their plans a secret until after Maud's grandmother died. The couple was not in love, but they did respect one another. They eventually married in 1911.

Sadly, there was never again any of the fun or romance in Lucy Maud Montgomery's life that she gave to the rest of the world through her delightful books with Anne, the wonderful character who lived in the house with the green gables.

CHAPTER FIFTEEN

The Romantic Legend
of Perce Rock

No dates remain to verify the accuracy of this story, but really, in this case, such details just aren't important. This wonderful old tale is one of the most romantic legends in Canadian history.

OUR COUNTRY WAS JUST A COLONY WHEN YOUNG BLANCHE de Beaumont left her home in Normandy, France, to board a ship bound for Canada. Raymond de Nerac, the love of Blanche's life, was settled in the New World and had sent for her. The anticipation of marrying her beloved Raymond combined with the adventure of sailing to Canada were almost more excitement than the young woman could bear. She waited impatiently for the voyage to end.

One day in mid-July, the ship's captain made the welcome declaration: "Land ahoy!" North America's shores were dead ahead. Blanche's heart pounded in her chest. Before too long she'd be in Raymond's arms. The voyage had been long and difficult, but soon all the trials would seem worthwhile. She had never felt happier.

Tragically, the young woman's elation did not last.

The next morning, a lookout perched high up on one of the ship's masts called out to the captain that another craft was approaching. Could it be a welcoming committee? Sadly, it was nothing like that. This was a pirate ship set on raiding theirs. Surely the travellers hadn't come all this way only to be slaughtered within a few miles of safety.

But seconds later, when a cannonball ripped across the deck of their ship, they realized that their end was, indeed, very near. Before they knew it, the pirate ship had pulled alongside, and the villains were climbing aboard, ready to pillage. The terrible sounds of metal on metal cut the air as sword fights ensued between the pirates and the sailors.

Through it all, Blanche, clutching her wedding gown to her breast, crouched out of the way, hiding as best she could and hoping that the pirates would leave before they spotted her. Her hope was in vain.

The pirate captain was delighted when he saw her. He had only expected to loot the ship and be gone, but here was a marvellous bonus—a young woman, beautiful almost beyond belief. Instantly, he made up his mind that he must have her all for himself. When he saw the wedding gown, the evil man knew just exactly how he could do that. He would marry her—the very next day.

And so, as the sun rose the following morning and the pirate ship sailed into the Gulf of St. Lawrence, the pirates gathered on the ship's deck.

They would be witnesses to the nuptials. (Of course, they were also on hand in case the bride needed any "help" in saying the vows that would link her forever to their captain.) Surprisingly, though, the beautiful young woman, radiant in her luminous white gown, smiled as she walked purposefully across the ship's deck.

But at the moment she should've stopped at her groom's side, Blanche ran to the ship's railing and threw herself into the sea. She'd smiled so happily that she'd fooled the men and they'd relaxed their guard. Not one of them was able to reach out in time to catch her. As they ran to the spot where she'd jumped, all that was left to see of the bride was a bit of filmy white trim from her gown. Then the deep, dark waters swallowed that up, too.

The pirate captain was devastated and enraged. He could barely command the ship. That night, they drifted aimlessly into a dense fog. Soon the vessel was completely enshrouded. When the mist lifted, the ship was dangerously close to an enormous monolith of rock jutting out of the water.

No one could ever remember seeing a rock there before. The men were frightened until they saw something strange on the rock. Then they were terrified. There before them, perched on top of the stone, was an image in white. An image they all recognized. It was Blanche—or her ghost. Worse, she was beckoning to them.

The men were frozen with fear.

Then, from the clear blue sky, a bolt of lightning slashed into the side of the pirate ship. None of the looters lived to tell the tale, but some say that if you look carefully at Perce Rock in the Gulf of St. Lawrence, you can still see traces of their ship embedded in the enormous boulder.

When the early morning light is just so and the fog clears a bit from around the rock, a beautiful young woman dressed in a glowing white gown appears at its summit. She seems to be floating, magically suspended, halfway between heaven and earth. Legend has it that this is the ghost of Blanche de Beaumont forever pining for her lost happiness.

And what of Raymond de Nerac? Sadly, the groom was also killed. He lost his life in a battle between the French and the Iroquois and died never knowing how close his bride had come to him before their deaths.

CHAPTER SIXTEEN

Lauretta Maracle and Tom Longboat
Fame, Wealth, Love and Mystery

In life, timing can be everything, and by coincidence alone, Tom Longboat's timing was excellent. The young man from the Six Nations reserve near Brantford, Ontario, was just a boy when the ancient Olympic games were revived in 1896. Of course, at the time, little Tom knew nothing about international sports. He just knew that he loved to run and that in foot races, he always came first.

IN OCTOBER 1906, LONGBOAT WAS 19 YEARS OLD. JUST FOR the fun of competing, he entered a race farther afield than those held on the reserve. The Hamilton Around the Bay Race was a gruelling 19 miles long. In addition to Tom, 25 other men were courageous enough to enter. Dozens more bravely placed bets on the race's outcome. The odds-on favourite was a man named John Marsh. Few bothered to pay any attention to the scrawny native kid in old canvas shoes who wore a jersey over a bathing suit. Those few who put money on the possibility of Tom Longboat winning the event were laughed at.

By the halfway point in the race, some runners had given up. Others, determined to finish, slogged along at a grinding pace. Only two men seemed to be enjoying themselves—the racers in first and second place. They were almost playing cat and mouse with each other—until the final few miles, that is. As the route wound its way up a hill, John Marsh slowed. Tom Longboat didn't. The youngster clearly had something left to give to the race. His determination kicked in like an overdrive gear, and Tom pulled away from his only true competition.

But his decision was nearly disastrous. He bolted in such a hurry that he took a wrong turn. Fortunately, the spectators lining the racecourse steered him back in the right direction. Even with his wrong turn and the time it took to correct the error, Tom Longboat crossed the finish line more than three minutes ahead of his nearest rival.

Everyone except Tom was surprised. Of course, the men who'd bet on the gangly Native kid were delighted—and richer by $1000, a significant amount of money in 1906. Tom left Hamilton that day with a roster of admirers and a head full of ideas. He began competing whenever he could, first in Toronto, then back in Hamilton, then across the border in Buffalo. He won most of the events he entered and attracted a lot of attention.

By the summer of 1908, Longboat had also attracted the eye of Lauretta Maracle, a Native woman seven years his senior. A few months later they were engaged, despite opposition from her family, who'd been informed that Longboat was "worthless." But Lauretta assured Tom that her family's opinion wasn't important in the least to her and that she just desperately wanted to be his wife till death do them part. Relieved, Tom headed to New York City for his next race—a much more impressive-looking runner, partly because Lauretta had sewn decorations onto his sharp new white running shorts.

That day, with Lauretta proudly in the stands cheering him on to victory, her fiancé, the man the press had by then dubbed "the fastest man in the world," ran to yet another win. Once the victory celebrations had faded away, Tom and Lauretta began to plan their wedding. On Monday, December 28, 1908, in a Toronto Anglican church, the two exchanged their vows.

By this time, Tom was a celebrity, and the Longboats' wedding reception was a party that was open to the public. From descriptions of the entertainment, which reportedly included a troupe of comedy acrobats, a female impersonator and several speeches, one of which was partly in Gaelic, the event must have resembled a vaudeville show more than a wedding reception! Hopefully the newlyweds enjoyed themselves at the gala, because less than a week later, Tom was entered in another race—a race that he won.

The young man was on top of the world. He was 21 years old, famous, wealthy and married to a beautiful woman. What more could anyone ask for? A photograph of Tom taken at that time shows a very contented-looking, nattily dressed young man reclining in an expensive-looking chair, smoking a cigar.

He and Lauretta were happily living in an upscale Toronto neighbourhood. For a kid with a grade four education, he was certainly doing all right! Occasionally, after a victory, he would over-celebrate at a bar or pub, but he was young enough to be able to throw off the ensuing hang-over without damaging his training regime.

Then came the Great War. It changed everyone's lives, including Tom's. He enlisted, and not surprisingly, the army used the young man as a runner to carry messages from post to post along the battle lines. Some historians maintain that Tom was wounded more than once while running dis-patches, but others say he made it through the war completely unscathed. There is no one alive today who would know for certain which version of the story is the truth. We do know, however, that one report Lauretta received was definitely not the truth, for she was informed that her husband of almost 10 years had been killed in action.

As a result, Tom Longboat, very much alive, returned from the war to find that his wife had married another man! Some say he was justifiably furious, others that he took the news reasonably well in stride.

Whichever account is correct, in 1920, at the age of 33, Tom married Martha Silversmith.

But what of Lauretta Maracle? Little is known and even less remembered about the woman whose wedding to the celebrity runner Tom Longboat had been such a public spectacle. Until just a few years ago, the story that he had come home from the war to find her married to another man was accepted as fact. That legend was even embellished by indications that the two had discussed the situation calmly and had decided that it was best for all concerned if Tom simply walked away. And he did.

But is that the truth?

It may not be.

The most mundane of research resources (the phone book!) indicates that in 1920, the year Tom remarried, Lauretta was still using the name Longboat. To confuse matters even further, in 1952, Lauretta's death was announced using her birth name, Maracle. The final mystery lies in the fact that her obituary made reference to a son, Reginald, whose surname was given as Longboat.

There seems to be no doubt that Tom's return from the war was a complete surprise to Lauretta, but perhaps she hadn't actually remarried. Could Tom have come home from the war and not found his wife married, but in a compromising situation, especially for that era? Perhaps while Tom was away, she had simply become pregnant by another man. She certainly wouldn't have been the only woman ever to have found herself in that situation—a situation that might well have made Tom, or almost any man, angry enough to leave his wife.

Despite Reginald's surname, it's extremely doubtful that Longboat was his father.

Tom and Martha went on to have five children. According to all accounts, they were happily married and devoted parents. When questioned about the possibility of a half-brother, one of Tom's sons maintained that his father had never so much as mentioned another child.

In the end, the reality of what killed Tom and Lauretta's great Canadian romance is a secret that she, perhaps the only person who ever knew the truth, took to her grave with her more than 50 years ago.

CHAPTER SEVENTEEN

Marie and Charles La Tour
Till Death

In 1640, Marie left her home in France and arrived on Canadian soil to marry a man she'd never met. That wasn't really an unusual situation during those pre-confederation years. What makes Marie's case exceptional is that she was not only a 38-year-old single woman, but also of noble birth.

Charles de Saint-Étienne de La Tour had lived in Acadia (now New Brunswick, Nova Scotia and Prince Edward Island) since 1610. He'd even been married to a Mi'kmaq woman for a while. In 1640, though, La Tour sent one of his men back to France with instructions to find him a new wife. His directions were simple—find a woman who was both healthy and wealthy.

Marie not only filled the bill on both those counts, but as she was to prove, she was no shrinking violet.

CHARLES LA TOUR'S TITLE OF ACADIAN LIEUTENANT-GOVERNOR might have misled Marie into thinking that she would continue to live in luxury at Fort La Tour, for she brought fine china, delicate pottery, crystal goblets and other elegant belongings with her when she sailed across the Atlantic Ocean. When she arrived at her new home, a rough shack surrounded by wilderness, the poor woman must have quickly realized that titles meant little in the New World.

Even though the English and the French were not at war with one another in 1640, the situation Marie found as she settled in was far from peaceful. King Louis XIII had granted Charles La Tour control over Acadia. Unfortunately, the king had also said exactly the same thing to another man, Charles d'Aulnay. Not surprisingly, the two men were bitter rivals. So much for the pampered, serene existence Marie had been used to!

During one attack, d'Aulnay's ships barricaded Fort La Tour. Soon ammunition supplies ran low. Marie and Charles waited until after dark one night, then the noblewoman and her high-ranking husband hid away in a rowboat and made their way past the blockade. They rowed out to one of their own supply ships, which had just arrived from France. From there they sailed to Boston, where they armed themselves as effectively as they could before returning to Acadia to chase d'Aulnay's ships away from their home fort.

Both Marie and Charles La Tour survived the battle, but three of d'Aulnay's men didn't. Marie was certain that d'Aulnay would report those killings to the French king and so, to protect her husband and his position in Acadia, she immediately set sail back to France to plead his case.

She tried, but failed, to convince King Louis XIII that La Tour should be left in charge. Worse, Marie was ordered not to go back to Acadia to help her husband, nor even to send help to him.

Bravely, the woman ignored the royal orders and made her way to England, where she boarded a ship bound for Acadia. Marie paid the captain, a man named Bailey, to sail directly there as fast as he could. As it turned out, though, the journey was anything but direct. Once Bailey had Marie's money, there was really very little she could do to control the voyage. Bailey knew he would make more money if he stopped to fish and trade with other ships, and that is exactly what he did. Fully six months elapsed before Marie arrived on the shores of North America, and even then, the captain went to Boston first instead of Acadia.

But Marie was still determined to get help to her husband. With the assistance of three English ships, she finally made it back to Fort La Tour in December 1646. The little settlement was in desperate trouble. Supplies had run dangerously low. As soon as his wife was back at home, La Tour set out for Boston, where he planned to buy the supplies needed to fight off d'Aulnay's forces.

The man had no sooner left on his mission than three of his men deserted, went over to d'Aulnay's side and informed La Tour's rival that Marie was now guarding the inadequately armed fort by herself. At first the enemy simply waited, and then, when a small ship sailed into view, they correctly assumed that La Tour had sent it from Boston. The vessel contained emergency supplies intended to help Marie fend off the enemy and a letter from La Tour explaining when and how he would be getting home.

But d'Aulnay's men captured the ship, stole the supplies and attacked Fort La Tour. Marie—the French noblewoman, now in her mid-40s—held off the assault as long as she could. When the situation seemed hopeless, Marie agreed to surrender to her enemy as long as he would spare the men's lives.

D'Aulnay agreed to her concession, but once he was inside the gates of the fort, he immediately went back on his word. He forced Marie to watch while each one of her loyal supporters was executed. Then she was put in jail herself.

Still determined to somehow save her husband, Marie wrote a letter warning La Tour of the situation at the fort. She gave it to a Native who hated d'Aulnay and asked that the man somehow get the message to her husband. Her last desperate act was discovered, and just weeks later, Marie La Tour died in prison—some say of a broken heart. The life that had begun in France's royal court had ended in tragedy.

As Marie's husband made his way back from Boston, he heard the dreadful news that his wife was dead and his enemy now controlled Fort La Tour.

He changed his course away from Acadia and sailed to Québec City instead.

La Tour lived in Québec for several years, until he heard that d'Aulnay had drowned. Then he sailed back to France and asked to be reinstated as Acadia's leader. The court agreed, and the man returned to his old fort at last.

Then, perhaps to ensure there'd never be any further trouble from anyone associated with his former enemy, La Tour married d'Aulnay's widow! The happy couple soon became parents and lived together until La Tour's death in 1666.

Poor Marie. All her efforts to fight against the d'Aulnay family apparently had been for naught!

Heartbeats

When Charles Vance Millar died on Halloween night in 1926, he left a very scary will. Millar had been a lawyer and a lifelong bachelor. As far as anyone knew, the man never had any children. Oddly, he bequeathed the bulk of his estate to the woman in Toronto who had the most babies over the following 10 years. In no time at all, word of this strange potential inheritance began to spread. Women all over the city suddenly became greedily amorous. The race to reproduce was on.

Members of the media were delighted. The best human interest story in years had just fallen into their typewriters. Newspaper readers' and radio audiences' appetites for updates were insatiable. And, considering the Dirty Thirties was not an era with a lot of good news, the attention was understandable.

While ordinary citizens were making love, local lawyers were arguing. Such a will could not be upheld, some barristers pronounced. Millar's relatives argued that they should inherit the man's money. In the end, the will was followed exactly as it had been written. Four women, each of whom had given birth to nine children, split the money.

At least one other woman, possibly two, earned a tenth of what those winners received for the 10 children they had produced during the decade. Their reduced share was said to have been because of paternity questions.

But the kicker is, Millar's strange legacy was actually meant to draw attention to the idiocy of the government's ban on the distribution of birth control information.

CHAPTER EIGHTEEN

Marion Mackintosh and Frederick Haultain
Better to Have Loved and Lost

In 1884, Frederick Haultain, an energetic and well-educated young man, moved west to open a law practice. Before long, the man was also involved with local politics. By 1887, he was premier of the Northwest Territories—the area we know today as the provinces of Saskatchewan and Alberta.

At the time, Charles Mackintosh was the Lieutenant-Governor of that same area. In what could have been a happy coincidence, Haultain was a bachelor and Mackintosh had a house-full of pretty daughters.

THE YOUNG LAWYER WAS PARTICULARLY SMITTEN WITH one Mackintosh daughter, Marion. And, judging from a newspaper description of her, it's no wonder. Marion apparently had "looked a poem" at a particular gala ball. An unnamed reporter noted "her tall, splendid figure" and that she carried herself "with perfect grace." But perhaps it was Marion's dress that attracted the most attention. The "bodice, pointed and very short, was cut quite low," its "fragile ending of chiffon about the throat gave a dainty finish."

That same journalist also noted that Marion Mackintosh and Frederick Haultain shared a dance that evening. But it would seem that Haultain was too wrapped up in his political career to pursue this lovely woman. He hesitated—and lost—without really even entering the race. Soon Marion was wed to a prosperous liquor merchant named Louis Alfred Castellain.

Three years later, in 1899, public opinion turned heavily against the consumption of alcohol, and Castellain's business failed. The man approached his wife's father, the Lieutenant-Governor, hoping for some sort of job with the government. But Mackintosh must have been a hard-hearted man, because even though he knew that Marion was in poor health, he turned his son-in-law away.

The Castellains fled to England, but if anything, their fortunes were worse there. Marion became pregnant, and her health deteriorated even more. When the baby, a girl, was born, she too was sickly. Castellain responded to these pressures by deserting his wife and child.

In 1902, Frederick Haultain sailed to England for the coronation of Edward VII. Apparently he still carried a torch for Marion, because he decided to visit her while he was there. The man was shocked by the way he found his former heart-throb. Marion and her daughter were living in hopeless squalor.

Haultain did what he could to make the woman and child comfortable while he was there. As soon as he was back in Canada, he arranged a meeting with the Lieutenant-Governor. He told Mackintosh about the terrible living conditions that his daughter and granddaughter were forced to endure, but Marion's father didn't offer any help. Haultain, horrified at the man's response, or lack of it, didn't have the heart to turn away from the destitute woman. For the next two years, he sent her a regular monthly allowance.

Then, in 1904, still living in London, Marion met another man—a potential husband. She followed her suitor to the United States and set about getting a divorce, at which point that man also deserted her. Haultain came to her rescue again, but this time she said she couldn't accept any further money from him unless they married.

Haultain was ecstatic. In 1906, at the age of 49, Frederick Haultain finally married Marion Mackintosh Castellain, the woman he'd been in love with, and had supported, for years. The couple kept the marriage a secret, though, because in those days marrying a divorcee was considered scandalous—certainly not the sort of behaviour that voters approved of from one of their leaders. The secrecy probably wasn't too much of a hardship for Haultain, because he'd already agreed to let Marion and her daughter go back to England for the next year. Announcing a marriage with no evidence of a wife might cause talk.

Sadly, that year in England came and went with no sign of Marion moving back to Canada. As a matter of fact, even her letters to Haultain became increasingly rare. Through it all, the man faithfully supported both Marion and her daughter even though he was not a wealthy man. Haultain confessed to a friend once that the money he sent his wife meant that sometimes he wasn't able to pay his own bills. But perhaps even more difficult to bear than the financial burden was the terrible disappointment Haultain must have felt at never being able to live with Marion as a normal husband and wife would.

By 1910, four years after they were married, it seemed as though Marion was finally healthy enough to return to Canada. No way was Haultain going to let his political career distract him this time. He resigned from politics so that he could devote all his time to looking after his wife whose mental and physical health were, by then, extremely fragile.

The man needn't have bothered resigning. Marion and her daughter finally did leave England for Canada but never managed to get any farther west than Ontario. Throughout it all, Frederick Haultain faithfully sent money.

By the time Marion died in 1938, Haultain had been supporting her for 36 years, 32 of those as her husband. Since their marriage, the two had never lived closer than several thousand kilometres apart, and for much of the unhappy union, they had not even lived on the same continent.

Few people ever knew that the two were even married. Official political registers don't mention Haultain's wife. Marion's burial records refer to her as Marion Castellain. Theirs was almost a phantom marriage, and yet it was real—especially in the amount of hardship it inflicted on Haultain's life.

By today's standards, it seems as though Marion played the generous, if naïve, man for a sucker, but perhaps they were both merely victims of her ill health and society as it was structured at that time. It was definitely one of the most tragic of all Canadian love stories.

Even if his long marriage to Marion Mackintosh had precious few happy moments, Haultain's life did have a happy ending. Not long after Marion passed away, he married again. Haultain and his second wife lived together until his death in 1942.

Frederick Haultain's long career of service to the burgeoning nation of Canada is still held in high regard.

Heartbeats

Day after day, 17-year-old Miana watched in horror as Nazi soldiers marched into the streets of the tiny village of Piccione, Italy, where she lived with her parents. Would anyone or anything ever be able to put an end to the relentless invasion of her beloved country? At last that country's much-needed rescuers came— Canadian soldiers ready to do battle until the Germans were forced to retreat. Within weeks there was victory. Italy had been liberated from the Nazi occupation! The Italians rejoiced and celebrated. From that moment on Canadian troops would rightly be regarded as heroes.

But those troops were, of course, made up of individual soldiers, young men who had left prairie farms, Maritime ports and growing Canadian cities—places they might never have left in their lifetimes had it not been for the war. Yes, they had accomplished heroic deeds, but for the most part, they were still just scared young men hoping to stay alive long enough to get back to the lives they'd left.

One of those men was Bob Hewitt, a member of the Elgin Regiment. He was just 23 years old in 1944. Despite the gratitude and hospitality the Italians showed the soldiers, Bob was achingly homesick. When they could, he and his friends would visit local families and attend community dances. It was through this socializing that young Hewitt met the 17-year-old Miana. She spoke only Italian. He spoke only English. But language didn't seem to be an issue between them.

At Christmas that year, he gave her toothpaste and a toothbrush—scarce items during those days of rations. Miana gave Bob a scarf she had knitted for him. In a small, quiet way, a romance was blossoming. Even after his regiment left her village, Bob managed to get back to visit Miana—once. Then a year and a half later, the young man was finally shipped home. He took the lovingly made scarf with him.

Once back on Canadian soil, Bob Hewitt gratefully rejoined the life that the war had interrupted. Less than a year later he married—not Miana from Piccione, but Helen from Cape Breton Island. Bob and his Canadian wife raised five children and enjoyed a long, happy marriage.

In 2004, the 60th anniversary of the liberation of Italy, Bob and many other veterans made a pilgrimage back to the place where they'd fought so hard and felt so scared and alone. Bob Hewitt took a side trip—a sentimental journey to Piccione.

As he walked through the familiar streets, the villagers went about their lives. First one and then another recognized him. "You were Miana's boyfriend," one man recalled. Bob met Miana's son and daughter, her neighbours and her friends, but not Miana herself.

The girl that Bob Hewitt had enjoyed a cross-cultural romance with, whose kindness had comforted him in his homesickness, had died in 1981, at the age of 54, fully 23 years before he'd been able to return and say goodbye properly. Hopefully she died knowing how important she'd been to the life of one young soldier.

CHAPTER NINETEEN

Janet Jones and Wayne Gretzky
The Great Romance

We loved him.

From the very first time Canadians saw him play, they were so proud that one of their own had proven to be, hands down, the finest player ever to lace up a pair of hockey skates. That gawky, awkward-looking 17-year-old youngster could definitely play our national game like no one else we'd ever seen.

Wayne Gretzky was simply the best.

We loved him extra well because he was just so Canadian. He was polite and respectful to everyone, on the ice and off. His family meant the world to him, and he lived year round in the hockey-mad city of Edmonton. For a few years he even dated a local girl. And he led Peter Pocklington's Edmonton Oilers to four Stanley Cups in five years.

During those years, Wayne Gretzky was asked to perform many off-ice duties. He always obliged, willingly and with class. He promoted local charities, visited children's hospitals, played in celebrity golf tournaments and once, in 1981, he was even asked to be a judge for a dance competition. A pretty dancer and actress named Janet Jones was also there. Whether it was because they were

both involved with other people at the time or simply that
Cupid failed to show up, there were no fireworks between
Wayne and Janet at that first meeting.

THE FATES WERE CONSPIRING, THOUGH, AND BY COINCIDENCE,
the two young people bumped into one another
several times over the next few years. Then in
1987, they met again, this time at a basketball
game. Before the last point had been scored,
Wayne Gretzky and Janet Jones were in love.

Canadians were delighted. Hockey's superstar-of-
all-time was going to marry a beautiful Hollywood
actress. We could hardly wait to fall in love with her,
too. And the ceremony! Why, it would be as close
to a royal wedding as we were ever likely to see.

The big day, July 16, 1988, finally arrived. VIPs,
hockey stars and movie moguls all dressed in
their finest smiled as they made their way up the
stairs of Edmonton's St. Joseph's Basilica. Janet
sneaked in a side door, later saying that she didn't
want anyone to see her wearing her delicate V-neck
white bridal gown before Wayne did. Gretzky
showed his usual class by telling a reporter that
the most important people in the church were his
grandmothers.

When the newlyweds stepped out of the church
after the ceremony to wave at the crowds gathered
on the sidewalks, it was clear that Gretzky had
brought yet another gift to Edmonton and Canadians
everywhere—his beautiful wife, Janet. She won

our hearts with her radiance and her obvious ado-
ration of our boy Wayne. What a happy day!

Then, less than three weeks later, the elation
came crashing down. The unthinkable had happened. Gretzky had been traded! Worse, he'd been
traded to a California team—as unlikely and
unnatural a place for hockey as surfing might be in
Edmonton.

After Canadians had recovered from the initial
trauma of a tearful Gretzky's announcement that
he would be leaving Edmonton to play for the Los
Angeles Kings, we immediately knew exactly who
to blame for our loss. (And establishing blame was
somehow important.) It was obviously the evil
bride's fault! Clearly, she wanted to continue her
career, and that was something she certainly couldn't
do in Edmonton. She'd need to be near Hollywood,
and given that she'd married hockey's best player,
he could "work" anywhere there was an NHL team.

Janet Jones had done the unthinkable, and in
doing so, had stomped all over the Canadian
hearts she'd just recently won. And so the situation stood for several days.

Canadian sportswriters were busier than they'd
been in a very long time. Anyone who was anyone, and many who were not, had things to say
about "the Trade."

Gretzky's former team mates certainly had a lot
to say to the press, and surprisingly, none of their
negative comments were directed towards Janet.

Those in the know, it seemed, were lashing out straight at Oilers owner Peter Pocklington. And, as was his style, he fired right back. This trade was what Gretzky wanted, Pocklington insisted. Now Canadians were even more sure that Janet was to blame for our heartbreaking loss.

How wrong we were.

Few people knew that at the time of their wedding, Wayne and Janet were thrilled with the fact that she was already pregnant. They both hoped to have a large family, and Janet very much looked forward to devoting herself full time to simply being a mother. Those were her career plans. She was most assuredly not in anyway responsible for the fact that her husband was leaving Canada. As a matter of fact, she'd been planning to settle down and live in Edmonton.

Finally, when she couldn't take the lies and rumours about herself and her husband one moment longer, Janet Jones Gretzky made a call to a sportswriter with an Edmonton newspaper. She needed to set the record straight. The next morning, the rest of the world knew the truth.

It seems that the day after Gretzky had led the Oilers to yet another Stanley Cup victory, Pocklington called the Great One to tell him that he was going to be traded. It was strictly a business deal and had nothing to do with what Janet did or didn't want.

Since then, Gretzky, our proudest export, has continued to prove not only that he's an exceptionally classy guy, but also that he continues to be a proud Canadian. As for the beautiful young woman he married in 1988, well, her behaviour has certainly made us eat all those terrible words we were saying about her less than a month after the wedding. Janet Jones Gretzky has kept such a low profile that it's often been difficult to keep track of how many children the couple has. (For those keeping score at home, there are five little Gretzkys— Paulina, Ty, Trevor, Tristan and Emma.)

Janet has been at Wayne's side for every one of the landmark occasions in his life since their marriage. She evidently enjoyed his victories as coach of Team Canada and was right there beside him with their children as he made his "farewell tour" around Edmonton's Coliseum when he retired as a hockey player. Janet is not a Jezebel, and Canada's royal wedding was not a farce.

Whew!

CHAPTER TWENTY

Signora Giorgia and William Lyon Mackenzie King
King of Romance

No book of Canadian romance stories would be complete without at least a nod to our own, very strangely romantic, Prime Minister William Lyon Mackenzie King. Even though he never married, it seemed that Mackenzie King, or Rex, as he preferred to be called, was always in love with someone or another. And sometimes those romances were in addition to the constant loves of his life—his mother and Joan Patteson, his neighbour's wife!

KING'S FONDNESS FOR HIS FATHER INCREASED CONSIDERABLY after the older man's death in 1916 and every year that followed. By 1934, Mackenzie King had become fond enough of his father that he decided to commission a sculpture of himself with his late father. King would sit for the sculpture himself, but for his father's likeness, the artist would have to work from a photograph.

Apparently there wasn't a sculptor in Canada whose work King admired sufficiently to hire for the job, so he travelled to Italy where he sat for an artist named Professor Guastalla. There was a language barrier between the two men, but fortunately

Guastalla had a neighbour who was willing to act as a translator. Her name was Signora Giorgia Borra de Cousandier.

Giorgia was 24 years of age. King was 59. The age difference between the two didn't seem to matter. They were immediately attracted to one another. One historian described Giorgia as a "handsome" woman. As there are no pictures available, that description will have to suffice. She was also an intelligent young woman, a lawyer's daughter and well educated in her own right.

Giorgia was also married.

Despite her marital status, Giorgia once confessed that she would have moved to Canada to be Mackenzie King's wife, if only he'd asked her. He didn't, though he did note in his journals that he was very attracted to her. By the time King was ready to leave Italy, the couple had been out for drives alone together in the Italian countryside.

The following year, Prime Minister King wrote to Giorgia and expressed his concern about Italy's invasion of Ethiopia. He explained to her that she, and the time they had enjoyed together, accounted in large part for his interest in Italy.

Then, in 1937, when Giorgia's third child died shortly after birth, King wrote to her again expressing his condolences for her loss. He closed that letter with a wish that the two of them could somehow be together again as they had been in the sculptor's studio.

By 1942, Giorgia's marriage had dissolved, partly, she later confessed, because of her relationship with Mackenzie King. When World War II ravaged Italy, Giorgia took King's letters with her every time she had to find safety in a bomb shelter. As Canadian prime minister, he ordered Allied troops to avoid using her home for military purposes. All this between a couple who had only known each other for a few days, more than a dozen years before.

It wasn't until 1946, when King was in Paris representing Canada at the Peace Conference, that the two long-distance lovers were able to see each other again. By all accounts they had a wonderful few days together before they returned to their home countries. King was by then 72 years of age, in poor health and world-weary. He sought the solace of his home and the care of his beloved Joan Patteson.

Right to the end, though, Giorgia was never far from King's mind. He dictated a letter to her just three days before his death in July 1952. She received it a month later, which meant that the man she once thought she wanted to marry had said goodbye to her from beyond the grave.

Signora Giorgia Borra de Cousandier lived in Italy for the rest of her life. She did find romance again, this time with an Italian journalist whom she eventually married.

Heartbeats

What woman doesn't like to look her best—especially when there's a mood of romance in the air. Very often the look she's after is achieved with a little illusion in the form of makeup. Where would modern romance be without the cosmetics industry and all its subtle, and not so subtle, tricks?

As admiration for Florence Nightingale and her selfless dedication to nursing spread throughout the world, parents began naming their newborn daughters in the woman's honour. That is how, in 1882, Mr. and Mrs. Graham of Vaughan Township in Ontario happened to name their second child not just Florence but Florence Nightingale Graham.

In her late teens, the young woman set out to fulfill the destiny her parents had created when they named her—Florence enrolled in nursing school. It wasn't long, though, before she realized that the work, the long hours and the financial rewards were in complete opposition to her lifelong dream. Hers was a lofty goal, yet elegantly simple. The Grahams' daughter wanted to be rich—extremely rich. In fact, she wanted to be the wealthiest woman in the world. And making sick people well just wasn't going to cut it where earning scads of cash was concerned.

Flo decided instead that she would make women beautiful.

She began to experiment with different lotions and potions. She soon realized that in order to really make it big, she'd have to leave her Canadian home. She settled in New York City, where she met Elizabeth Hubbard. Together they set about revolutionizing the cosmetics industry so that women looking for romance could look their very best. The partnership between the two soon made the name Elizabeth Arden popular with women all over the world. And in doing so, created an enormously profitable business.

Graham and Hubbard's partnership didn't last, but the company certainly did, and Florence Graham adopted the name Elizabeth Arden as her own. Then she added "Mrs." for respectability's sake. Sadly, though, a lasting marriage eluded the cosmetics queen. Although she married twice, neither union was a happy one.

Despite her marital troubles, Elizabeth Arden eventually realized the goal that little Florence Nightingale Graham had set for herself years before. When she died in 1965, the woman who helped other women look their best was fabulously wealthy.

Notes on Sources

Beddoes, Dick. *Pal Hal*. Markham, Ontario: Penguin Books, 1989.

Boulton, Marsha. *Just a Minute More*. Toronto: McArthur and Company, 1999.

Boulton, Marsha. *Just a Minute Omnibus*. Toronto: McArthur and Company, 2000.

Cowley, George and Deborah Cowley. *One Woman's Journey: A Portrait of Pauline Vanier*. Outremont, Québec: Novalis, 1992.

Dion, Celine (Georges-Hebert Germain). *Celine Dion: My Story, My Dream*. Toronto: Harper Collins, 2000.

Edmonton Journal. March 25 and November 2, 2004.

Fetherling, Douglas, ed. *The Broadview Book of Canadian Anecdotes*. Peterborough, Ontario: Broadview Press, 1998.

Fisher, Charles, ed. *Dearest Emilie: The Love-Letters of Sir Wilfrid Laurier to Madame Emilie Lavergne*. Toronto: NC Press, 1989.

Grills, Barry and Jim Brown. *Celine Dion: A New Day Dawns*. Kingston, Ontario: Fox Music Books, 2004.

Hancock, Pat. *Canadian Trivia 2*. Toronto: Scholastic Books, 2005.

Johnston, Gordon. *It Happened in Canada*. Richmond Hill: Scholastic Publishing, 1984.

La Giorgia, Giancarlo. *Canadian War Heroes: Ten Profiles in Courage*. Edmonton: Folklore Publishing, 2005.

MacEwan, Grant. *Marie Anne: The Frontier Spirit of Marie Anne Lagimodiere*. Saskatoon: Western Producer Prairie Books, 1984.

McCoy, Deborah. *The World's Most Unforgettable Weddings: Love, Lust, Money and Madness*. New York: Citadel Press, 2001.

Peacock, Shane. *Unusual Heroes: Canada's Prime Ministers and Fathers of Confederation*. Toronto: Puffin Canada, 2002.

Podnieks, Andrew. *The Great One: The Life and Times of Wayne Gretzky*. Toronto: Doubleday Canada, 1999.

Robertson, Heather. *More Than a Rose: Prime Ministers Wives and Other Women*. Toronto: Seal Books, 1991.

Seagrave, Kerry. *Politicians' Passions: The Love Affairs of the World's Most Powerful Men*. New York: SPI Books, 1992.

Smith, Barbara. *Passion & Scandal: Great Canadian Love Stories*. Calgary, Alberta: Detselig Enterprises, 1997.

Smith, Barbara. *Ontario Ghost Stories, Volume II*. Edmonton: Ghost House Books, 2002.

Smith, Barbara. *Ghost Stories of the Rocky Mountains*. Edmonton: Lone Pine Publishing, 1999.

Smith, Beverley. *Gold on Ice: The Sale and Pelletier Story*. Toronto: Key Porter Books, 2002.

Taylor, Jim. *Wayne Gretzky: The Authorized Pictorial Biography*. Vancouver: Whitecap Books, 1994.

Toronto Sunday World. October 16, 1921.

Trotier, Maxine. *Canadian Explorers*. Toronto: Scholastic Books, 2005.

Trudeau, Margaret. *Beyond Reason*. New York: Simon & Schuster, 1979.

Vancouver Sun. October 13, 1987.

Waite, P.B. *Late Harvest: Mackenzie King and The Italian Lady*. *The Beaver*. December 1995/January 1996, Volume 75:6.

Wojna, Lisa. *Canadian Inventions: Fantastic Feats & Quirky Contraptions*. Edmonton: Folklore Publishing, 2004.

Barbara Smith

Barbara Smith has always collected folklore and has successfully combined it with her other passion, writing. A bestselling author of more than 20 books, she has a deep interest in social history and loves historical research so much that she'd rather "research than eat." She has taught creative writing courses at the university and college level and is a charismatic public speaker. Barbara and her husband Bob currently live in Edmonton, Alberta.

Here are more great titles from the GREAT CANADIAN STORIES series from Folklore Publishing...

CANADIAN WOMEN ADVENTURERS: Stories of Daring and Courage
by Tamela Georgi and Lisa Wojna

This entertaining and informative book chronicles the fascinating exploits of strong Canadian women who influenced the course of Canada's history. Read about mountaineer Sharon Wood, astronaut Roberta Bondar, journalist Faith Fenton, artist Emily Carr and many others who have pioneered new horizons for women.

$9.95 CDN • ISBN10: 1-894864-39-5 • ISBN13: 978-1-894864-39-8 • 5.25" x 8.25" • 144 pages

GREAT CANADIAN WOMEN:
Nineteen Portraits of Extraordinary Women
by Lisa Wojna

This book honours the legacy and continuing struggle of women of talent and courage who, from all walks of life and vocations, have contributed significantly to Canada's evolution. Among those featured are Marion Orr, who ferried fighter planes to England during World War II and established flight schools in Ontario; Louise Arbour, the controversial Supreme Court Justice who was appointed United Nations High Commissioner for Human Rights in 2004; Anne Murray, known as "Canada's Songbird" and the first Canadian artist to have an American gold record; Barbara Frum, the dedicated newscaster and journalist for CBC Radio who pioneered the popular and influential current affairs program *As It Happens*; and Charlotte Whitton, the brash and colourful mayor of Ottawa, the first woman to hold such an office in Canada.

$9.95 CDN • ISBN10: 1-894864-47-6 • ISBN13: 978-1-894864-47-3 • 5.25" x 8.25" • 160 pages

PIONEER CANADIAN ACTORS:
The Stories Behind Legends of the Silver Screen
by Stone Wallace

This book celebrates the Canadian men and women who showed the world that some of the most impressive acting talent comes from Canada. Learn about the careers of Donald Sutherland, Lorne Green, Christopher Plummer, Mary Pickford, William Shatner and more.

$9.95 CDN • ISBN10: 1-894864-42-5 • ISBN13: 978-1-894864-42-8 • 5.25" x 8.25" • 144 pages

BILLIONAIRES OF CANADA
by Tim le Riche

This book profiles some of Canada's wealthiest people, from their beginnings in business to the peak of their success and, sometimes, their downfall. Among those featured are the Bronfman family, which built its fortune selling booze during Prohibition; Jimmy Pattison, the car salesman with a drive to succeed in everything from advertising to groceries; the McCain family, which went from small potatoes to the world's largest french fry manufacturers; and Bernard Ebbers, who knew the heights as CEO of WorldCom until he became a convicted criminal.

$9.95 CDN • ISBN10: 1-894864-56-5 • ISBN13: 978-1-894864-56-5 • 5.25" x 8.25" • 144 pages

Look for books in the *Great Canadian Stories* series at your local bookseller and newsstand or contact the distributor, Lone Pine Publishing, directly. In Canada, call 1-800-661-9017.